THE BHAGAVAD GITA

★

On this path effort never goes to waste,
and there is no failure. Even a little effort
toward spiritual awareness will protect you
from the greatest fear. (2:40)

The Bhagavad Gita

★

Translated with a general introduction by

EKNATH EASWARAN

With chapter introductions by Diana Morrison

NILGIRI PRESS

©1985 by the Blue Mountain Center of Meditation
All rights reserved. Printed in the United States of America
Designed, printed, and bound by Nilgiri Press
ISBN: cloth, 0–915132–36–2 paper, 0–915132–35–4

Eighth printing January 1996

The Blue Mountain Center of Meditation, founded in Berkeley,
California, in 1961 by Eknath Easwaran, publishes books on
how to lead the spiritual life in the home and the community.

For information please write to
Nilgiri Press, Box 256, Tomales, California 94971

Library of Congress Cataloging in Publication Data
will be found on the last page of this book

Table of Contents

Introduction

The Bhagavad Gita

MANY YEARS AGO, when I was still a graduate student, I traveled by train from central India to Simla, then the summer seat of the British government in India. We had not been long out of Delhi when suddenly a chattering of voices disturbed my reverie. I asked the man next to me if something had happened. "Kurukshetra!" he replied. "The next stop is Kurukshetra!"

I could understand the excitement. Kurukshetra, "the field of the Kurus," is the setting for the climactic battle of the Mahabharata, the vastest epic in any world literature, on which virtually every Hindu child in India is raised. Its characters, removed in time by some three thousand years, are as familiar to us as our relatives. The temper of the story is utterly contemporary; I can imagine it unfolding in the nuclear age as easily as in the dawn of Indian history. The Mahabharata is literature at its greatest—in fact, it has been called a literature in itself, comparable in its breadth and depth and characterization to the whole of Greek literature or Shakespeare. But what makes it unique is that embedded in this literary masterpiece is one of the finest mystical documents the world has seen: the Bhagavad Gita.

I must have heard the Gita recited thousands of times when I was growing up, but I don't suppose it had any special significance for me then. Not until I went to college and met Mahatma Gandhi did I begin to understand why nothing in the long, rich stretch of Indian culture has had a wider appeal, not only within India but outside as well. Today, after more than thirty years of devoted study, I would not hesitate to call it India's most important gift to the world. The Gita has been translated into every major language and perhaps a hundred times into English alone; commentaries on it are said to be more numerous than on any other scripture. Like the Sermon on the Mount, it has an immediacy that sweeps away time, place, and circumstance. Addressed to everyone, of whatever background or status, the Gita distills the loftiest truths of India's ancient wisdom into simple, memorable poetry that haunts the mind and informs the affairs of everyday life.

Everyone in our car got down from the train to wander for a few minutes on the now peaceful field. Thousands of years ago this was Armageddon. The air rang with the conch-horns and shouts of battle for eighteen days. Great phalanxes shaped like eagles and fish and the crescent moon surged back and forth in search of victory, until in the end almost every warrior in the land lay slain.

"Imagine!" my companion said to me in awe. "Bhishma and Drona commanded their armies here. Arjuna rode here, with Sri Krishna himself as his charioteer. Where you're standing now—who knows?—Arjuna might have sat, his bow and arrows on the ground, while Krishna gave him the words of the Bhagavad Gita."

The thought was thrilling. I felt the way Schliemann must have when he finally reached that desolate bluff of western Turkey and knew he was standing "on the ringing plains of windy Troy," walking the same ground as Achilles, Odysseus, Hector, and Helen. Yet at the same time, I felt I knew the setting of the Gita much more intimately than I could ever know this peaceful field. The battlefield is a perfect backdrop, but the Gita's subject is the war within, the struggle for self-mastery that every human being must wage if he or she is to emerge from life victorious.

Historians surmise that like the Iliad, the Mahabharata might well be based on actual events, culminating in a war that took place somewhere between 1000 and 700 B. C.—close, that is, to the very dawn of recorded Indian history. This guess has recently been supported by excavations at the ancient city of Dvaraka, which, according to the Mahabharata, was destroyed and submerged in the sea after the departure of its divine ruler, Krishna. Only five hundred years or so before this, by generally accepted guess, Aryan tribes originally from the Caucasus had invaded the Indian subcontinent and imposed their martial civilization on the peoples they found, bringing the prototype of the Sanskrit language and countless elements of belief and culture that have been part of the Hindu tradition ever since. The oldest part of the most ancient of Hindu scriptures, the Rig Veda, dates from this period—about 1500 B.C., if not earlier.

Yet the real sources of Indian religious faith, I believe, must be traced to a much earlier epoch. When the Aryans entered the Indian subcontinent through the mountains of the Hindu Kush, they encountered a civilization on the banks of the Indus river that archeologists date back as far as 3000 B. C. Roughly contemporaneous with the pyramid-builders on the Nile, these Indus-dwellers achieved a comparable level of technology. They had metalworks skilled in sheet-making, riveting, and casting of copper and bronze, crafts and industries with standardized methods of production, land and sea trade with cultures as far away as Mesopotamia, and well-planned cities with water supply and public sanitation systems unequaled until the Romans. Evidence suggests that they may have used a decimal system of measurement. But most remarkable, it is

apparently here and not with the Aryans that the great
spiritual discoveries of Hinduism originated. Images of
Shiva as Yogeshvara, the Lord of Yoga, suggest that
meditation was practiced in a civilization which
flourished a millenium before the Vedas were committed to an oral tradition.

If this is so, it would imply that the same systematic
attitude the Indus Valley dwellers applied to their technology was applied also to study of the mind. This was
brahmavidya, the "supreme science"–supreme because
where other sciences studied the external world,
brahmavidya sought knowledge of an underlying reality which would inform all other studies and activities.

Whatever its origins, in the early part of the first
millenium B. c. we find clearly stated both the methods
and the discoveries of brahmavidya. With this introspective tool the inspired *rishi*s (literally "seers") of
ancient India analyzed their awareness of human experience to see if there was anything in it that was absolute.
Their findings can be summarized in three statements
which Aldous Huxley, following Spinoza, has called
the Perennial Philosophy because they appear in every
age and civilization: (1) there is an infinite, changeless
reality beneath the world of change; (2) this same reality
lies at the core of every human personality; (3) the purpose of life is to discover this reality experientially: that
is, to realize God while here on earth. These principles
and the interior experiments for realizing them were
taught systematically in "forest academies" or
ashrams–a tradition which continues unbroken after
some three thousand years.

The discoveries of brahmavidya were systematically
committed to memory (and eventually to writing) in
the Upanishads, visionary documents that are the earliest and purest statement of the Perennial Philosophy.
How many of these precious records once existed no
one knows; some 108 have survived as part of the

Hindu canon of authority, the four Vedas. All have one unmistakable hallmark: the vivid stamp of personal mystical experience. These are records of direct encounter with the divine. Tradition calls them *shruti*: literally "heard," as opposed to learned; they are their own authority. By convention, only the Vedas (including their Upanishads) are considered shruti, based on direct knowledge of God.

According to this definition, all other Indian scriptures—including the Gita—are secondary, dependent on the higher authority of the Vedas. However, this is a conventional distinction and one that might disguise the nature of the documents it classifies. In the literal sense the Gita too is shruti, owing its authority not to other scriptures but to the fact that it set down the direct mystical experience of a single author. Shankara, a towering mystic of the ninth century A.D. whose word carries the authority of Augustine, Eckhart, and Aquinas all in one, must have felt this, for in selecting the minimum sources of Hinduism he passed over almost a hundred Upanishads of Vedic authority to choose ten central Upanishads and the Bhagavad Gita.

The Gita, I would argue, is not an integral part of the Mahabharata. It is essentially an Upanishad, and my conjecture is that it was set down by an inspired seer (traditionally Vyasa) and inserted into the epic at the appropriate place. Other fragments seem to have been added in this way to the Mahabharata and to other popular secondary scriptures; it is an effective way of preserving new material in an oral tradition. There is also traditional weight behind this idea, for as far back as anyone can trace, each chapter of the Gita has ended with the same formula: "In the Bhagavad-Gita Upanishad, the text on the supreme science [*brahmavidya*] of yoga, this is the chapter entitled. . . ."

Finally, by way of further support, we can observe that except for its first chapter, which sets the stage, the

Gita not only does not develop the action of the Mahabharata but is rather at odds with it. Battle lines are drawn—the climax of decades of dissension—and on the eve of combat, prince Arjuna loses his nerve and asks his charioteer, Krishna, what to do. Then what? Krishna—no ordinary charioteer, but an incarnation of God—enters into some seven hundred verses of sublime instruction on the nature of the soul and its relation to God, the levels of consciousness and reality, the makeup of the phenomenal world, and so on, culminating in a stupendous mystical experience in which he reveals himself to Arjuna as the transcendent Lord of life and death. He counsels Arjuna to be compassionate to friend and enemy alike, to see himself in every person, to suffer others' sorrows as his own. Then the Gita is over, the narration picks up again, and battle is joined—a terrible, desperate slaughter compromising everyone's honor, by the end of which Arjuna's side emerges victorious but almost every man of fighting age on both sides has been slain. Only great genius would have placed the Gita in such a dramatic setting, but it stands out from the rest as a timeless, practical manual for daily living.

To those who take this dramatic setting as part of the spiritual instruction and get entangled in the question of the Gita justifying war, Gandhi had a practical answer: just base your life on the Gita sincerely and systematically and see if you find killing or even hurting others compatible with its teachings. (He makes the same point of the Sermon on the Mount.) The very heart of the Gita's message is to see the Lord in every creature and act accordingly, and the scripture is full of verses to spell out what this means:

> I am ever present to those who have realized me in
> every creature. Seeing all life as my manifestation, they
> are never separated from me. They worship me in the

hearts of all, and all their actions proceed from me.
Wherever they live, they abide in me. (6:30–31)

When a person responds to the joys and sorrows
of others as if they were his own, he has attained the
highest state of spiritual union. (6:32)

That one I love who is incapable of ill will, who is
friendly and compassionate . . . who looks upon friend
and foe with equal regard. . . . (12:13)

He alone sees truly who sees the Lord the same in every
creature, who sees the deathless in the hearts of all that
die. Seeing the same Lord everywhere, he does no harm
to himself or others. Thus he attains the supreme goal.
(13:27–28)

Scholars can debate the point forever, but when the Gita
is practiced, I think, it becomes clear that the struggle
the Gita is concerned with is the struggle for self-
mastery. It was Vyasa's genius to take the whole great
Mahabharata epic and see it as metaphor for the perennial war between the forces of light and the forces of
darkness in every human heart. Arjuna and Krishna are
then no longer merely characters in a literary masterpiece. Arjuna becomes Everyman, asking the Lord
himself, Sri Krishna, the perennial questions about life
and death—not as a philosopher, but as the quintessen-
tial man of action. Thus read, the Gita is not an external
dialogue but an internal one: between the ordinary human personality, full of questions about the meaning of
life, and our deepest Self, which is divine.

There is, in fact, no other way to read the Gita and
grasp it as spiritual instruction. If I could offer only one
key to understanding this divine dialogue, it would be
to remember that it takes place in the depths of consciousness and that Krishna is not some external being,
human or superhuman, but the spark of divinity that
lies at the core of the human personality. This is not
literary or philosophical conjecture; Krishna says as

much to Arjuna over and over: "I am the Self in the heart of every creature, Arjuna, and the beginning, middle, and end of their existence" (10:20).

In such statements the Gita distills the essence of the Upanishads, not piecemeal but comprehensively, offering their lofty insights as a manual not of philosophy but of everyday human activity—a handbook of the Perennial Philosophy unique in world history.

THE UPANISHADIC BACKGROUND

The Gita, naturally enough, takes for granted that its audience is familiar with the basic ideas of Hindu religious thought, almost all of which can be found in the Upanishads. It also uses some technical vocabulary from yoga psychology. All this needs to be explained in contemporary terms if the modern reader is to grasp what is essential and timeless in the Gita's message and not get bogged down in strange terminology.

First, however, the non-Hindu faces a third obstacle: the multiplicity of names used for aspects of God. From the earliest times, Hinduism has proclaimed one God while accommodating worship of him (or her, for to millions God is the Divine Mother) in many different names. "Truth is one," says a famous verse of the Rig Veda; "men call it by various names." A monastic devotee might find that Shiva embodies the austere detachment he seeks; a devotee who wants to live "in the world," partaking of its innocent pleasures but devoted to service of his fellow creatures, might find in Krishna the perfect incarnation of his ideals. In every case, this clothing of the Infinite in human form serves to focus a devotee's love and to provide an inspiring ideal. But whatever form is worshipped, it is only an aspect of the same one God.

In the Gita—in fact, virtually everywhere in Hindu myth and scripture—we also encounter "the gods" in the plural. These are the *deva*s, deities which seem to have come in with the Aryans and which have recognizable counterparts in other Aryan-influenced cultures: Indra, god of war and storm; Varuna, god of waters and a moral overseer; Agni, god of fire, the Hermes-like intermediary between heaven and earth; and so on. The Gita refers to the devas as being worshipped by those who want to propitiate natural and supernatural powers, in much the same way that ancestors were worshipped. In modern terms, they can best be understood as personifying the forces of nature.

This question out of the way, we can proceed to the Upanishadic background the Gita assumes.

Atman and Brahman

The Upanishads are not systematic philosophy; they are more like ecstatic slide shows of mystical experience—vivid, disjointed, stamped with the power of direct personal encounter with the divine. If they seem to embrace contradictions, that is because they do not try to smooth over the seams of these experiences. They simply set down what the rishis saw, viewing the ultimate reality from different levels of spiritual awareness, like snapshots of the same object from different angles: now seeing God as utterly transcendent, for example, now seeing God as immanent as well. These differences are not important, and the Upanishads agree on their central ideas: *Brahman,* the Godhead; *Atman,* the divine core of personality; *dharma,* the law that expresses and maintains the unity of creation; *karma,* the web of cause and effect; *samsara,* the cycle of birth and death; *moksha,* the spiritual liberation that is life's supreme goal.

Even while ancient India was making breakthroughs in the natural sciences and mathematics, the sages of the Upanishads were turning inward to analyze the data that nature presents to the mind. Penetrating below the senses, they found not a world of solid, separate objects but a ceaseless process of change—matter coming together, dissolving, and coming together again in a different form. Below this flux of things with "name and form," however, they found something changeless: an infinite, indivisible reality in which the transient data of the world cohere. They called this reality Brahman: the Godhead, the divine ground of existence.

This analysis of the phenomenal world tallies well enough with contemporary physics. A physicist would remind us that the things we see "out there" are not ultimately separate from each other and from us; we perceive them as separate because of the limitations of our senses. If our eyes were sensitive to a much finer spectrum, we might see the world as a continuous field of matter and energy. Nothing in this picture resembles a solid object in our usual sense of the word. "The external world of physics," wrote Sir Arthur Edding- ton, "has thus become a world of shadows. In remov- ing our illusions we remove the substance, for indeed we have seen that substance is one of the greatest of our illusions." Like the physicists, these ancient sages were seeking an invariant. They found it in Brahman.

In examining our knowledge of ourselves, the sages made a similar discovery. Instead of a single coherent personality, they found layer on layer of components— senses, emotions, will, intellect, ego—each in flux. At different times and in different company, the same per- son seems to have different personalities. Moods shift and flicker, even in those who are emotionally stable; desires and opinions change with time. Change is the nature of the mind. The sages observed this flow of thoughts and sensations and asked, "Then where am *I?*" The parts do not add up to a whole; they just flow by. Like physical phenomena, the mind is a field of forces, no more the seat of intelligence than radiation or gravity is. Just as the world dissolves into a sea of energy, the mind dissolves into a river of impressions and thoughts, a flow of fragmentary data that do not hold together.

Western philosophers have reasoned their way to a similar conclusion, but with them it was intellectual exercise. David Hume confesses that whenever he was forced to conclude his empirical ego was insubstantial, he went out for a walk, had a good dinner, and forgot all about it. For these ancient sages, however, these were not logical conclusions but personal discoveries. They were actually exploring the mind, testing each level of awareness by withdrawing consciousness to the level below. In profound meditation, they found, when consciousness is so acutely focused that it is utterly withdrawn from the body and mind, it enters a kind of singularity in which the sense of a separate ego disappears. In this state, the supreme climax of meditation, the seers discovered a core of consciousness beyond time and change. They called it simply Atman, the Self.

I have described the discovery of Atman and Brahman—God immanent and God transcendent—as separate, but there is no real distinction. In the climax of meditation, the sages discovered *unity*: the same indivisible reality without and within. It was *advaita,* "not two." The Chandogya Upanishad says epigrammatically, *Tat tvam asi*: "Thou art That." Atman *is* Brahman: the Self in each person is not different from the Godhead.

Nor is it different from person to person. The Self is one, the same in every creature. This is not some peculiar tenet of the Hindu scriptures; it is the testimony of everyone who has undergone these experiments in the depths of consciousness and followed them through to the end. Here is Ruysbroeck, a great mystic of medieval Europe; every word is most carefully chosen:

The image of God is found essentially and personally in all mankind. Each possesses it whole, entire and un-divided, and all together not more than one alone. In this way we are all one, intimately united in our eternal image, which is the image of God and the source in us of all our life.

Maya

In the unitive experience, every trace of separateness disappears; life is a seamless whole. But the body cannot remain in this state for long. After a while, awareness of mind and body returns, and then the conventional world of multiplicity rushes in again with such vigor and vividness that the memory of unity, though stamped with reality, seems as distant as a dream. The unitive state has to be entered over and over until a person is established in it. But once established, even in the midst of ordinary life, he sees the One underlying the many, the Eternal beneath the ephemeral.

What is it that makes undivided reality appear to be a world of separate, transient objects? What makes each of us believe that we are the body rather than our own Self? The sages answered with a story still told after thousands of years. Imagine, they said, a man dreaming that he is being attacked by a tiger. His pulse will race, his fists will clench, his forehead will be wet with the dew of fear—all just as if the attack were real. He will be able to describe the look of his tiger, the way he smelled, the sound of his roar. For him the tiger is real, and in a sense he is not wrong: the evidence he has is not qualita-tively different from the kind of evidence we trust when we are awake. People have even died from the phys-iological effects of a potent dream. Only when we wake up can we realize that our dream-sensations, though real to our nervous system, are a lower level of reality than the waking state.

The Upanishads delineate three ordinary states of

consciousness: waking, dreaming, and dreamless sleep. Each is real, but each has a higher order of reality. For beyond these three, the Upanishads say, is the unitive state, called simply "the fourth": *turiya*. Entering this state is similar to waking up out of dream sleep: the individual passes from a lower level of reality to a higher one.

The sages called the dream of waking life—the dream of separate, merely physical existence—by a suggestive name, *maya*. In general use the word meant a kind of magic, the power of a god or sorcerer to make a thing appear to be something else. In the Gita maya becomes the creative power of the Godhead, the primal creative energy that makes unity appear as the world of innumerable separate things with "name and form."

Later philosophers explained maya in surprisingly contemporary terms. The mind, they said, observes the so-called outside world and sees its own structure. It reports that the world consists of a multiplicity of separate objects in a framework of time, space, and causality because these are the conditions of perception. In a word, the mind looks at unity and sees diversity; it looks at what is timeless and reports transience. And in fact the percepts of its experience *are* diverse and transient; on this level of experience, separateness is real. Our mistake is in taking this for ultimate reality, like the dreamer thinking that nothing is real except his dream.

Nowhere has this "mysterious Eastern notion" been formulated more succinctly than in the epigram of Ruysbroeck: "We behold what we are, and we are what we behold." When we look at unity through the instruments of the mind, we see diversity; when the mind is transcended, we enter a higher mode of knowing—turiya, the fourth state of consciousness—in which duality disappears. This does not mean, however, that the phenomenal world is an illusion or unreal. The illusion is the sense of separateness.

Here again we can illustrate from physics: the world of "name and form" exists only as a condition of perception; at the subatomic level, separate phenomena dissolve into a flux of energy. The effect of maya is similar. The world of the senses *is* real, but it must be known for what it is: unity appearing as multiplicity.

The person who disidentifies himself with the conditions of perception in maya wakes up into a higher mode of knowing in which the unity of life is apprehended directly. The disciplines for achieving this are called yoga, as is the state of union: the word comes from the root *yuj,* to yoke or bind together. The "experience" itself (properly speaking, it is beyond experience) is called *samadhi.* And the state attained is *moksha* or *nirvana,* both of which signify going beyond the conditioning of maya—time, space, and causality.

In this state the individual realizes that he is not a physical creature but the Atman, the Self, and thus not separate from God. He sees the world not as pieces but whole, and he sees that whole as a manifestation of God. Once identified with the Self, he knows that although his body will die, *he* will not die; his awareness of this identity is not ruptured by the death of the physical body. Thus he has realized the essential immortality which is the birthright of every human being. To such a person, the Gita says, death is no more traumatic than taking off an old coat (2:13,22).

Life cannot offer any higher realization. The supreme goal of human existence has been attained. The man or woman who realizes God has everything and lacks nothing: "Having this, one desires nothing further; he cannot be shaken by the heaviest burden of sorrow" (6:22). Life cannot threaten such a person; all it holds is the opportunity to love, to serve, and to give.

Dharma, Karma, Rebirth, and Liberation

It has been said that if you understand just two words,

dharma and *karma,* you will have grasped the essence of Hinduism. This is a simplification, but it would be difficult to exaggerate the importance of these concepts. Both are deeply embedded in Hindu thought, and the Gita, like other Hindu scriptures, takes them for granted, not as theoretical premises but as facts of life that can be verified in personal experience.

The word *dharma* means many things, but its underlying sense is "that which supports," from the root *dhri,* to support, hold up, or bear. Generally *dharma* implies support from within: the essence of a thing, its virtue, that which makes it what it is.

An old story illumines this meaning with the highest ideal of Hinduism. A sage, seated beside the Ganges, notices a scorpion that has fallen into the water. He reaches down and rescues it, only to be stung. Some time later he looks down and sees the scorpion thrashing about in the water again. Once more he reaches down to rescue it, and once more he is stung. A bystander, observing all this, exclaims, "Holy one, why do you keep doing that? Don't you see that the wretched creature will only sting you in return?" "Of course," the sage replied. "It is the dharma of a scorpion to sting. But it is the dharma of a human being to save."

On a larger scale, *dharma* means the essential order of things, an integrity and harmony in the universe and the affairs of life that cannot be disturbed without courting chaos. Thus it means rightness, justice, goodness, purpose rather than chance.

Underlying this idea is the oneness of life: the Upanishadic discovery that all things are interconnected because at its deepest level creation is indivisible. This oneness bestows a basic balance on the whole of nature such that any disturbance in one place has to send ripples everywhere, as a perfect bubble, touched lightly in one place, trembles all over until balance is restored. The implications are caught perfectly by those famous lines from Donne, which deserve to be read now with a fresh eye as not merely great rhetoric but a faithful representation of reality:

> No man is an island, entire of itself; every man is a piece of the continent, a part of the main; if a clod be washed away by the sea, Europe is the less, as well as if a promontory were, as well as if a manor of thy friends or of thine own were; any man's death diminishes me, because I am involved in mankind; and therefore never send to know for whom the bell tolls, it tolls for thee.

There is an ancient Sanskrit epigram, *Ahimsa paramo dharma*: the highest dharma is *ahimsa,* nonviolence, universal love for all living creatures; for every kind of violence is a violation of dharma, the fundamental law of the unity of life.

Thus every act or thought has consequences, which themselves will have consequences; life is the most intricate web of interconnections. This is the law of karma, one of the most important and least understood ideas in ancient Indian thought. *Karma* is repeated so often in the Gita that I want to illustrate it in some detail: some intuitive sense of karma as an organic law makes Krishna's teachings a good deal clearer.

Literally, the Sanskrit *karma* means something that is done. Often it can be translated as "deed" or "action." The law of karma states simply that every event is both a cause and an effect. Every act has consequences of a similar kind, which in turn have further consequences and so on; and every act, every karma, is also the consequence of some previous karma.

This refers not only to physical action but to mental activity as well. In their analysis of the phenomenal world and the world within, the sages of the Upanishads found that there is not merely an accidental but an essential relationship between mental and physical activity. Given appropriate conditions to develop

16

further, thoughts breed actions of the same kind, as a seed can grow only into one particular kind of tree.

Baldly put, the law of karma says that whatever you do will come back to you. If Joe hits Bob, and later Ralph hits Joe, that is Joe's karma coming back to him. This sounds occult because we do not see all the connections; but the connections are there, and the law of karma is no more occult than the law of gravitation. It states that that blow has to have consequences; it cannot end with Bob getting a black eye. It makes an impression on Bob's consciousness—predictably, he gets furious—and it makes an impression on Joe's consciousness as well.

Let us trace it first through Bob. He might take revenge on Joe then and there, simply by hitting him back: that is "cash karma," where you do something and pay for it immediately. In these times, however, it is more likely that Bob will suppress his feelings, so that the consequences of Joe's blow do not show up until later—probably in ways that seem to have nothing to do with Joe or his fist. Karma is rarely so simple as this illustration, but in any case it should be clear that Bob's anger at Joe will have repercussions throughout his relationships. Those repercussions will have repercussions—say, Bob goes home and explodes at his wife, and his wife gets angry at Ralph's wife, who takes it out on Ralph, who works with Joe; and the next time Joe irritates Ralph, Ralph lets him have it. Poor Joe, rubbing his chin, can't have the slightest idea that he is being repaid for hitting Bob. All he feels is anger at Ralph: and so the chain of consequences continues, and Joe's karmic comeuppance becomes the seed of a new harvest.

Most people have no idea how many others are affected by their behavior and example. It gives some idea of how complex the web of karma actually is. No one, of course, has the omniscience to see this picture fully. But the idea of a network of such connections, far from being occult, is natural and plausible. The law of karma states unequivocally that though we cannot see the connections, we can be sure that everything that happens to us, good and bad, originated once in something we did or thought. We ourselves are responsible for what happens to us, whether or not we can understand how. It follows that we can change what happens to us by changing ourselves; we can take our destiny into our own hands.

The physical side of karma, however—hitting and getting hit back—only touches the surface of life. To get an inkling of how karma really works, we have to consider the mind.

Everything we do produces karma in the mind. In fact, it is in the mind rather than the world that karma's seeds are planted. When Joe hits Bob, I said, there are effects on Bob's face and consciousness. But there are also effects on Joe's consciousness. For one, by indulging a hot temper, Joe has made it more likely that he will indulge that temper again. He is a little different because of his action; he has made himself an angrier person. Over the years, if he keeps giving in to his moods, he will grow more belligerent. He may find himself swinging his fists more and more often; and by some quirk of human nature, he will find himself in situations that cry out for fists to be swung. Sooner or later he will get into a fight where he is repaid in kind; that is one way in which his karma with Bob might be reaped.

The Buddha says that we are not punished for our anger; we are punished *by* our anger. Anger is its own karma. Joe may think he feels better for having hit Bob, but a physician would observe what happens while Joe is getting heated up—watch his blood pressure soar and his heart race, measure the adrenaline and other hormones dumped into the body, and so on—and conclude that he is putting himself under serious physiological stress. Even if Ralph never gets to hit him, Joe is hitting himself from inside. If his anger becomes chronic, he will live in a world of constant stress, predisposing him to heart disease, ulcer, migraine, and other physiological problems. These too are routes by which the karma of anger can be reaped.

Further, Joe's aggressiveness and irritability make him harder to live with. His relationships deteriorate. Perhaps his friends start to avoid him; perhaps his co-workers respond to him with increasing resentment. All of this is likely to provoke him even more. Life in such circumstances can be miserable, and Joe might find himself drinking or smoking heavily or seeking escape in high-risk activities like skydiving or stock car racing—all of which provide more ways in which karma can be reaped. The analysis could go on; these are only illustrations.

One more fascinating point about karma: even if Joe does not actually strike anybody, the karma of anger is still generated in the mind and body. To the extent he gets angry, his blood pressure will still shoot up, his stomach get tense, his heart race, and so on. Thoughts have concrete consequences: they shape the way we see life, which in turn affects our health, our behavior, our choice of work and friends—in short, everything we do.

Aptly, Indian philosophy compares a thought to a seed: very tiny, but it can grow into a huge, deep-rooted, wide-spreading tree. I have seen places where a seed in a crack in a pavement grew into a tree that tore up the sidewalk. It is difficult to remove such a tree, and terribly difficult to undo the effects of a lifetime of negative thinking, which can extend into many other people's lives. But it can be done, and the point of the Gita is to show how.

Karma is sometimes considered punitive, a matter of getting one's just deserts. This is accurate enough, but it is much more illuminating to consider karma an educative force whose purpose is to teach the individual to act in harmony with dharma—not to pursue selfish interests at the expense of others, but to contribute to life and consider the welfare of the whole. In this sense life is like a school; one can learn, one can graduate, one can skip a grade or stay behind. As long as a debt of karma remains, however, a person has to keep coming back for further education. That is the basis of *samsara,* the cycle of birth and death.

A good many wrong and misleading words have been written on this subject, largely because of the fascination it seems to hold in the West. Rightly understood, however, reincarnation is not exotic but quite natural. If personality consists of several sheaths, the body being only the outermost, there is no reason why personality should die when the body is shed. The sages of the Upanishads saw personality as a field of forces. Packets of karma to them are forces that have to work themselves out; if the process is interrupted by death, those forces remain until conditions allow them to work again in a new context.

Again, sleep can illustrate the dynamics of this idea. In sleep a person passes in and out of two stages, dreaming and dreamless sleep. In the first, consciousness is withdrawn from the body and senses but still engaged in the mind. In dreamless sleep, however, consciousness is withdrawn from the mind as well. Then the thinking process—even the sense of "I"—is temporarily suspended, and consciousness is said to rest in the Self. In this state a person ceases to be a separate creature, a separate personality. In dreamless sleep, the Upanishads say, a king is not a king nor a pauper poor; no one is old or young, male or female, educated or ignorant. When consciousness returns to the mind, however, the thinking process starts up again, and personality returns to the body.

According to this analysis, the ego dies every night. Every morning we pick up our desires where we left

off: the same person, yet a little different too. The Upanishads describe dying as a very similar process. Consciousness is withdrawn from the body into the senses,
from the senses into the mind, and finally consolidated
in the ego; when the body is finally wrenched away, the
ego remains, a potent package of desires and karma.
And as a person's last waking thoughts shape his
dreams, the contents of the unconscious at the time of
death—the residue of all that he has thought and desired
and lived for in the past—determine the context of his
next life. He takes a body again, the sages say, to come
back to just the conditions where his desires and karma
can be fulfilled. The Self-realized person, however, has
no karma to work out, no personal desires; at the time
of death he is absorbed into the Lord:

> But they for whom I am the supreme goal, who do all
> work renouncing self for me and meditate on me with
> single-hearted devotion, these I will swiftly rescue
> from the fragment's cycle of birth and death, for their
> consciousness has entered into me. (12:6–7)

Such a person, the Upanishads stress, can actually
shed his body voluntarily when the hour of death ar-
rives, by withdrawing consciousness step by step in full
awareness. Some of the Gita's most fascinating verses,
for those who can interpret them, are Krishna's instructions on how to die (8:12–13).

YOGA PSYCHOLOGY

In trying to describe their discoveries, the Upanishadic
seers developed a specialized vocabulary. Their terms
were later elaborated by mystics who were also brilliant
philosophers—Kapila, Shankara, and others, the ancient
Indian counterparts of men like Augustine and Aquinas
in the West. The most useful part of this vocabulary
comes from Sankhya, the philosophical system whose
practical counterpart is the school of meditation called

Yoga. Both are traditionally traced to one towering authority, Kapila, and have much in common with
Buddhist philosophy. An ancient saying celebrates their
practicality: "There is no theory like Sankhya, no practice like Yoga."

The Gita does not belong to the Sankhya school or to
any other; it is as comprehensive as the Upanishads. But
no philosophy provides a more precise vocabulary than
Sankhya for describing the workings of the mind, and
that vocabulary the Gita draws on freely.

Sankhya philosophy posits two separate categories:
Purusha, spirit, and *prakriti,* everything else. This is not
the Western mind-matter distinction. Prakriti is the
field of what can be known objectively, the field of
phenomena, the world of whatever has "name and
form": that is, not only of matter and energy but also of
the mind. As physics postulates a "unified field" of
energy from which all phenomena can be derived,
Sankhya describes a field that includes mental phenomena as well. Thus mind, energy, and matter are
points on a continuum—a field of forces. Purusha, pure
spirit, is the knower of this field of phenomena, and
belongs to a wholly different order of reality. Only
Purusha is conscious—or, rather, Purusha is consciousness itself. What we call "mind" is only an internal instrument that Purusha uses, just as the body is its external instrument. For practical purposes—at least as far as
the Gita is concerned—*Purusha* may be regarded as a
synonym for *Atman.* Purusha is the Self, beyond all
change, the same in every creature.

Matter and Mind

Perhaps I should confess at this point that the paragraphs in this short section are somewhat technical and
not necessary for understanding the Gita. They can be
skipped by anyone who finds them dry. I include them
simply because Sankhya's explanation of mind and

matter, when properly understood, makes scientific sense of many statements in the Gita that might otherwise seem arbitrary: maya, the survival of personality after death, the way karma works through the mind. It accommodates modern physics perfectly and offers promising explanations of mind–body relationships in health and disease. However, Sankhya's way of looking at the mind is very different from our usual physical orientation, and therefore impossible to absorb without reflection.

Sankhya's hallmark is a list (*sankhya* means counting or listing) of twenty-four principles or *tattva*s ("suchnesses") which trace the steps by which unitary, primordial prakriti becomes manifested as the countless forms of mind, matter, and energy that make up the world we live in. The tattvas are listed in the Gita:

> The field, Arjuna, is made up of the following: the five areas of sense perception; the five elements; the five sense organs, and the five organs of action; the three components of the mind: manas, buddhi, and ahamkara; and the undifferentiated energy [prakriti] from which all these evolved. (13:5)

I know of no English words to use for most of these twenty-four constituents. *Manas* corresponds roughly to "mind" the way that word is commonly used; *buddhi* is the discriminative faculty, the discriminating intellect; *ahamkara,* literally "I-maker," is the sense of ego. I have used such rough labels in the translation which follows, but really they are technical terms with precise definitions, each associated with a specific function and level of consciousness. Approximations are misleading because they bring in associations from Western philosophy, which has a wholly different orientation. Behind all these categories lies a powerful, practical assumption: Sankhya is not trying to describe physical reality; it is analyzing consciousness, knowledge, for the sole purpose of unraveling the human being's true identity. So it does not begin with the material universe as something different and separate from the mind that perceives it. It does not talk about sense objects outside us and senses within and then try to get the two together. It begins with one world of experience. Sense objects and senses are not separate; they are two aspects of the same event. Mind, energy, and matter are a continuum, and the universe is not described as it might be in itself, but as it presents itself to the human mind. As they say in the "new physics," it is not just an observable universe but a participatory universe.

Let me illustrate. This morning I had a fresh mango for breakfast: a large, beautiful, fragrant one which had been allowed to ripen until just the right moment, when the skin was luminous with reds and oranges. You can see from that kind of description that I like mangos. I must have eaten thousands of them when I was growing up, and I probably know most varieties intimately by their color, shape, flavor, fragrance, and feel.

Sankhya would say that this mango I appreciated so much does not exist in the world outside—at least, not with the qualities I ascribed to it. The mango-in-itself, for example, is not red and orange; these are categories of an eye and nervous system that can deal only with a narrow range of radiant energy. My dog Bogart would not see a luscious red and orange mango. He would see some gray mass with no distinguishing features, much less interesting to him than a piece of buttered toast. But my mind takes in messages from five senses and fits them into a precise mango-form in consciousness, and that form—nothing outside—is what I experience. Not that there is no "real" mango! But what I experience, the objects of my sense perception and my "knowing," are in consciousness, nowhere else. A brilliant neuroscientist I was reading recently says something similar in contemporary language: we never really encounter the world; all we can experience is our own nervous system.

When the Gita says that the material world is made up of five "material elements," then, it is talking about the world *as we perceive it through our five senses*. The objects of this world are in the mind, not outside. "Physical objects" in this sense require a mental component also: five "essences" or mental conditions of perception, each corresponding to one of the five senses. From these five *tanmatras* derive on the one hand the five sense organs, and on the other hand the five material elements. You can see that the number five and the correspondences of Sankhya are not arbitrary, but reflect the ways we have of sorting electrical information supplied to the brain.

Four of these elements have names similar to those from ancient philosophy in the West—earth, air, fire, and water. But if we remember that we are talking about principles of perception rather than "earth-stuff," "fire-stuff," and so on, it should become clear that this is not an antiquated theory left behind by the progress of physical science. It is quite sophisticated and accommodates contemporary physical thought rather well, for it recognizes that in the act of knowing, the mind conditions what is known.

Senses and sense objects, then, are very intimately related. There is a causal connection, for example, between the things we see and the physical organ of seeing, the eye and its related branches of the nervous system: both depend on the underlying form in the mind that conditions how we perceive light. The objects we see are shaped by the way we see. So senses and sense objects "make sense" only together: each is incomplete without the other. That is why there is such a strong pull between senses and sense objects.

On the other hand, the Gita says, this pull has nothing to do with us—the Self, the knower. When Krishna keeps telling Arjuna to train his mind to be alike in

pleasure and pain, he is simply being practical: to discover unity, consciousness has to be withdrawn from
the hold of the senses, which ties it to duality.

> When the senses contact sense objects, a person experi-
> ences cold or heat, pleasure or pain. These experiences
> are fleeting; they come and go. Bear them patiently,
> Arjuna. Those who are unaffected by these changes,
> who are the same in pleasure and pain, are truly wise
> and fit for immortality. (2:14–15)

The sensory attraction of pleasure is just an interaction
between inert elements of similar stuff, very much like a
magnetic pull between two objects. *We* are not involved. When I look at a fresh, ripe mango, it is natural
for my senses to respond; that is their nature. But I
should be able to stand aside and watch this interaction
with detachment, the way people stand and watch
while movers unload a van. In that way I can enjoy
what my senses report without ever having to act compulsively on their likes and dislikes.

Sankhya's explanation of mind and body has profound implications for psychosomatic medicine. I have
no space to elaborate here, but it should be clear that in a
system where mental phenomena and biochemical
events take place in the same field, it is much easier to
account for how ways of thinking affect the body. If one
idea is central to yoga psychology, it is that thoughts are
real and have real, tangible consequences, as should be
clear from the discussion of karma. Sankhya describes
thoughts as packets of potential energy, which begin to
grow more and more solid when favorable conditions
are present and obstacles are removed. They become
desires, then habits, then ways of living with physical
consequences. Those consequences may look no more
like thoughts than an oak tree looks like an acorn, but
the Gita says they are just as intimately related. Just as a
seed can grow into only one kind of tree, thoughts can

produce effects only of the same nature. Kindness to others, to take just one example, favors a nervous system that is kind to itself.

The Forces of Evolution

Sankhya describes prakriti as a field of forces called *gunas*—a concept that gets a good deal of attention in the Gita.

According to Sankhya, the evolution of primordial prakriti into mind and matter begins when the equilibrium of prakriti is disturbed. In Hindu myth this is the "dawn" of the Day of Brahma (8:17–21), a period of explosive expansion not unlike the Big Bang with which modern cosmology says the universe began. At this instant of creation, thrown into imbalance, prakriti differentiates itself into three basic states or qualities of primordial energy. These are the gunas. Every state of matter and mind is a combination of these three: *tamas,* inertia, *rajas,* activity, and *sattva,* harmony or equilibrium. These are only rough translations, for the gunas have no equivalent in any other philosophy I know.

The gunas can be illustrated by comparison with the three states of matter in classical physics: solid, liquid, and gas. Tamas is frozen energy, the resistance of inertia. A block of ice has a good deal of energy in the chemical bonds that hold it together, but the energy is locked in, bound up, rigid. When the ice melts, some of that energy is released as the water flows; rajas, activity, is like a swollen river, full of uncontrolled power. And sattva, harmony, can be compared with steam when its power is harnessed. These are very imprecise parallels, but they convey an important point about the gunas: all three are states of energy, and each can be converted into the others.

Guna means strand, and in the Gita the gunas are described as the very fabric of existence, the veil that hides unity in a covering of diversity. Tamas is maya's power of concealment, the darkness or ignorance that hides unitive reality; rajas distracts and scatters awareness, turning it away from reality toward the diversity of the outside world. Thus the gunas are essentially born of the mind. When the mind's activity is stilled, we see life as it is.

We can also think of the gunas as different levels of consciousness. Tamas, the lowest level, is the vast unconscious, a chaotic dumping ground for the residue of past mental states. "Unconscious" in this sense has something in common with Jung's collective unconscious, in that it is the repository not only of past experiences but also of our evolutionary heritage, the basic drives of the human being's animal past. This record is shared, of course, by all human beings, and at its deepest levels the unconscious is universal. There is no choice in tamas, no awareness; this is complete ignorance of the unity of life, ignorance of any other need than one's own basic urges.

Rajas is what we ordinarily mean by mind, the incessant stream of thought that races along desiring, worrying, resenting, scheming, competing, frustrating and getting frustrated. Rajas is power released, but uncontrolled and egocentric.

Sattva, finally, is the so-called higher mind—detached, unruffled, self-controlled. This is not a state of repressive regulation, but the natural harmony that comes with unity of purpose, character, and desire. Negative states of mind do still come up, prompted by tamas and rajas, but you do not have to act on them.

According to Sankhya, everything in the world of mind and matter is an expression of all three gunas, with one guna always predominant. This becomes particularly interesting in describing personality as a field of forces. The rajasic person is full of energy; the tamasic person is sluggish, indifferent, insensitive; the sattvic person, calm, resourceful, compassionate, and selfless. Yet all three are always present at some level of awareness, and their proportions change: their interplay is the dynamics of personality. The same individual will have times when he is bursting with energy and times when inertia descends and paralyzes his will, times when he is thoughtful and other times when he is moving so fast that he never notices those around him. The person is the same; he is simply experiencing the play of the gunas. As long as he identifies with his body and mind, he is at the mercy of this play. But the Self is not involved in the gunas' interaction; it is witness rather than participant:

> Without senses itself, it shines through the functioning of the senses. Completely independent, it supports all things. Beyond the gunas, it enjoys their play. (13:14)

The gunas form the basis of the most compassionate account of human nature I have come across in any philosophy or psychology, East or West. They not only explain differences in character; they describe the basic forces of personality and allow the possibility of reshaping ourselves after a higher ideal. Because personality is a process, the human being is constantly remaking himself. Left to itself, the mind goes on repeating the same old habitual patterns of personality. By training the mind, however, anyone can learn to step in and change old ways of thinking; that is the central principle of yoga:

> Reshape yourself through the power of your will; never let yourself be degraded by self-will. The will is the only friend of the Self, and the will is the only enemy of the Self. (6:5)

The Gita speaks of this kind of growth as part of spiritual evolution. In its natural state, consciousness is a continuous flow of awareness. But through the distorting action of the gunas, we have fallen from this native state into fragmented, sometimes stagnant awareness. Seeing through a divided mind, we see life divided wherever we look: separate selves, antagonistic interests, conflicts within ourselves. Evolution, according to the Gita, is a painfully slow return to our native state. First tamas must be transformed into rajas— apathy and insensitiveness into energetic, enthusiastic activity. But the energy of rajas is self-centered and dispersed; it must be harnessed to a higher ideal by the will. Then it becomes sattva, when all this passionate energy is channeled into selfless action. This state is marked by happiness, a calm mind, abundant vitality, and the concentration of genius.

But even this is not the end. The goal of evolution is to return to unity: that is, to still the mind. Then the soul rests in pure, unitary consciousness, which is a state of permanent joy.

> In the still mind, in the depths of meditation, the Self reveals itself. Beholding the Self by means of the Self, an aspirant knows the joy and peace of complete fulfillment. (6:20)

THE ESSENCE OF THE GITA

The Gita does not present a system of philosophy. It offers something to every seeker after God, of whatever temperament, by whatever path. The reason for this universal appeal is that it is basically practical: it is a handbook for Self-realization and a guide to action.

Some scholars will find practicality a tall claim, because the Gita is full of lofty and even abstruse philosophy. Yet even its philosophy is not there to satisfy intellectual curiosity; it is meant to explain to a spiritual aspirant why he is asked to undergo certain disciplines. Like any handbook, the Gita makes most sense when it is practiced.

As the traditional chapter titles put it, the Gita is

30

Brahmavidyayam yogashastra, a textbook on the supreme science of yoga. But *yoga* is a word with many meanings—as many, perhaps, as there are paths to Self-realization. What kind of yoga does the Gita teach?

The common answer is that it presents three yogas or even four—the four main paths of Hindu mysticism. In *jnana yoga,* the yoga of knowledge, an aspirant uses his will and discrimination to disidentify himself from his body, mind, and senses until he knows he is nothing but the Self. The follower of *bhakti yoga,* the yoga of devotion, achieves the same goal by identifying himself completely with the Lord in love; by and large, this is the path taken by most of the mystics of Christianity, Judaism, and Islam. In *karma yoga,* the yoga of selfless action, the aspirant dissolves his identification with body and mind by identifying with the whole of life, forgetting his finite self in the service of others. And the follower of *raja yoga,* the yoga of meditation, disciplines his mind and senses until the mind-process is suspended in a healing stillness and he merges in the Self.

Indians like to classify, and the eighteen chapters of the Gita are said to break into three six-chapter parts. The first third, according to this, deals with karma yoga, the second with jnana yoga, and the last with bhakti yoga: that is, the Gita begins with the way of selfless action, passes into the way of Self-knowledge, and ends with the way of love. This scheme is not tight, and non-Hindu readers may find it difficult to discover in the text. But the themes are there, and Krishna clearly shifts his emphasis as he goes on using this one word *yoga.* Here he focuses on transcendental knowledge, there on selfless action, here on meditation, there on love.

Thus the Gita offers something for every kind of spiritual aspirant, and for two thousand years each of the major schools of Indian philosophy has quoted the Gita in defense of its particular claims. This fluidity some-

times exasperates scholars, who feel the Gita contra-
dicts itself. It also puzzled Arjuna, the faithful repre-
sentative of you and me. "Krishna," he says at the beginning of Chapter 3, "you've been telling me that
knowledge [jnana] is better than action [karma]; so why
do you urge me into such terrible action? Your words
are inconsistent; they confuse me. Tell me *one* path to
the highest good" (3:1–2). No doubt he speaks for every
reader at this point, and for those who go on wanting
one path only, the confusion simply grows worse.

For those who try to practice the Gita, however,
there is a thread of inner consistency running through
Krishna's advice. Like a person walking around the
same object, the Gita takes more than one point of
view. Whenever Krishna describes one of the traditional paths to God he looks at it from the inside, extolling
its virtues over the others. For the time being, that is *the*
path; when he talks about yoga, he means that one particular yoga. Thus "this ancient word" yoga, says Gandhi's intimate friend and secretary, Mahadev Desai,

> is pressed by the Gita into service to mean the entire
> gamut of human endeavor to storm the gates of heaven.
> . . . [It means] the yoking of all the powers of the body
> and the mind and soul to God; it means the discipline
> of the intellect, the mind, the emotions, the will, which
> such a yoking presupposes; it means a poise of the soul
> which enables one to look at life in all its aspects
> and evenly.

The Gita brings together all the specialized senses of the
word *yoga* to emphasize their common meaning: the
sum of what one must do to realize God.

The thread through Krishna's teaching, the essence of
the Gita, can be given in one word: renunciation. This is
the common factor in the four yogas. It is a bleak word
in English, conjuring up the austerity and self-
deprivation enjoined on the monastic orders—the

"poverty, chastity, and obedience" so perfectly embodied by Francis of Assisi. When the Gita promises "freedom through renunciation," the impression most of us get is that we are being asked to give up everything we want out of life; in this drab state, having lost whatever we value, we will be free from sorrow. Who wants that kind of freedom?

But this is not at all what the Gita means. It does not even enjoin material renunciation, although it certainly encourages simplicity. As always, its emphasis is on the mind. It teaches that we can become free by giving up not material things but selfish attachments to material things—and, more important, to people. It asks us to renounce not the enjoyment of life but the clinging to selfish enjoyment whatever it may cost others. It pleads, in a word, for the renunciation of selfishness in thought, word, and action—a theme that is common to all mystics, West and East alike.

Mahatma Gandhi encapsulates the Gita's message in one phrase: *nishkama karma,* selfless action, work free from any selfish motives. In this special sense, whatever path the Gita is presenting at a given time, it remains essentially a manual of karma yoga, for it is addressed to the person who wants to realize God without giving up an active life in the world. In the Gita the four traditional yogas are not watertight compartments, and in practice, all of them blend and support each other on the path to Self-realization.

Nishkama karma means literally work that is without *kama,* that is, without selfish desire. This word *kama*—indeed the whole idea of desire in Hindu and Buddhist psychology—is frequently misunderstood. These religions, it is sometimes held, teach an ideal of desireless action, a nirvana equated with the extinction of all desires. This drab view is far from the truth. Desire is the fuel of life; without desire nothing can be achieved, let alone so stupendous a feat as Self-realization. *Kama* is not desire; it is selfish desire. The Buddha calls it *tanha*, "thirst": the fierce, compulsive craving for personal satisfaction that demands to be slaked at any cost, whether to oneself or to others. Thus the concept also includes what Western mystics call self-will—the naked ego insisting on getting what it wants for its own gratification. The Gita teaches simply that this selfish craving is what makes a person feel separate from the rest of life. When it is extinguished—the literal meaning of *nirvana*—the mask of the transient, petty empirical ego falls, revealing our real Self.

Work hard in the world without any selfish attachment, the Gita counsels, and you will purify your consciousness of self-will. In this way any man or woman can gradually attain freedom from the bondage of selfish conditioning.

This is a *mental* discipline, not just a physical one, and I want to repeat that to understand the Gita, it is important to look beneath the surface of its injunctions and see the mental state involved. *Nishkama karma* is not "good works" or philanthropic activity; work can benefit others and still carry a good measure of ego-involvement. Such work *is* good, but it is not yoga. It may benefit others, but it will not necessarily benefit the doer. Everything depends on the state of mind. Action without selfish motive purifies the mind: the doer is less likely to be ego-driven later. The same action done with a selfish motive entangles a person further, precisely by strengthening that motive so it is more likely to prompt selfish action again.

In the Gita this is said in many ways, and from differences in language it may seem that Krishna is giving different pieces of advice. In practice, however, it becomes evident that these are only various ways of saying the same thing.

To begin with, Krishna often tells Arjuna to "renounce the fruits of action" (*karma-phala*):

You have the right to work, but never to the fruit of work. You should never engage in action for the sake of reward, nor should you long for inaction. Perform work in this world, Arjuna, as a man established within himself—without selfish attachments, and alike in success and defeat. For yoga is perfect evenness of mind. (2:47–48)

"Fruits," of course, means the outcome. What Krishna means is to give up attachment to the results of what you do: that is, to give your best to every undertaking without insisting that the results work out the way you want, or even whether what you do is pleasant or unpleasant. "You have the right to action, but not to the fruits of action": each of us has the obligation to act rightly, but no power to dictate what is to come of what we do. Mahatma Gandhi explains with the authority of his personal experience:

> By detachment I mean that you must not worry whether the desired result follows from your action or not, so long as your motive is pure, your means correct. Really, it means that things will come right in the end if you take care of the means and leave the rest to Him.

"But renunciation of fruit," Gandhi warns,

> in no way means indifference to the result. In regard to every action one must know the result that is expected to follow, the means thereto, and the capacity for it. He who, being thus equipped, is without desire for the result and is yet wholly engrossed in the due fulfillment of the task before him, is said to have renounced the fruits of his action.

This attitude frees a person completely. Whatever comes—success or failure, praise or blame, victory or defeat—he can give his best with a clear, unruffled mind. Nothing can shake his courage or break his will; no setback can depress him or make him feel "burned out."

Clearly, as the Gita says, "Yoga is skill in action" (2:50).

Only the person who is utterly detached and utterly dedicated, Gandhi says, is free to enjoy life. Asked to sum up his life "in twenty-five words or less," he replied, "I can do it in three!" and quoted the Isha Upanishad: "Renounce and enjoy." The person who is compulsively attached to the results of action cannot really enjoy what he does; he gets downcast when things do not work out and clings more desperately when they do. So the Gita classifies the karma of attachment as "pleasant at first, but bitter poison in the end" (18:37), because of the painful bondage of conditioning.

Again, Krishna repeatedly tells Arjuna to surrender everything to him in love. But this is not different advice, merely different words. Krishna is asking Arjuna to act entirely for His sake, not for any personal gain. The whole point of the path of love is to transform motivation from "I, I, I" to "thou, thou, thou"— that is, to surrender selfish attachments by dissolving them in the desire to give.

Krishna puts this most beautifully in the famous verses of Chapter 9 which begin, "Whatever you do, make it an offering to me" (9:27). Do it, that is, not for personal reward but out of love for the Lord, present in every creature. "Whatever you eat, whatever worship you perform, whatever you give, whatever you suffer": everything is to be done and given and endured and enjoyed for the sake of the Lord in all, not for ourselves. *Manmana*: this is the refrain of the Gita. Krishna tells Arjuna repeatedly, "Fill your mind with me, focus every thought on me, think of me always"; then "you will be united with me" (cf. 9:34). The same injunction was given to Moses and reiterated by Jesus and Mohammed. In practical terms, it means that awareness will be integrated down to the deepest recesses of the unconscious, which is precisely the significance of the word *yoga*.

Meister Eckhart says eloquently of this state:

> Whoever has God in mind, simply and solely God, in all things, such a man carries God with him into all his works and into all places, and God alone does all his works. He seeks nothing but God; nothing seems good to him but God. He becomes one with God in every thought. Just as no multiplicity can dissipate God, so nothing can dissipate this man or make him multiple.

Thus we arrive at the idea of "actionless action": of persons so established in identification with the Self that in the midst of tireless service of those around them, they remain in inner peace, the still witness of action. *They* do not act, the Gita says; it is the Self that acts through them: "They alone see truly who see that all actions are performed by prakriti, while the Self remains unmoved" (13:29). Again, this is a universal testimony. Here is one of the most active of mystics, St. Catherine of Genoa:

> When the soul is naughted and transformed, then of herself she neither works nor speaks nor wills, nor feels nor hears nor understands; neither has she of herself the feeling of outward or inward, where she may move. And in all things it is God who rules and guides her, without the mediation of any creature. And the state of this soul is then a feeling of such utter peace and tranquility that it seems to her that her heart, and her bodily being, and all both within and without, is immersed in an ocean of utmost peace. . . . And she is so full of peace that though she press her flesh, her nerves, her bones, no other thing comes forth from them than peace.

Again, when the Gita talks about "inaction in the midst of action" (4:18, etc.), we can call on Ruysbroeck to illuminate the seeming paradox. The person who has realized God, he says, mirrors both His aspects: "tranquility according to His essence, activity according to

His nature: absolute repose, absolute fecundity." And he adds,

> The interior person lives his life according to these two ways; that is to say, in rest and in work. And in each of them he is wholly and undividedly; for he dwells wholly in God in virtue of his restful fruition and wholly in himself in virtue of his active love. . . . This is the supreme summit of the inner life.

This is the only kind of inaction the Gita recommends. It is action of the most tireless kind; the only thing inactive is the ego. To live without the daily sacrifice (*yajna*) of selfless service—to work just for oneself, or worse, to do nothing at all—is simply to be a thief (3:12). It is not possible to do nothing, Krishna says; the very nature of the mind is incessant activity. The Gita's goal is to harness this activity in selfless service, removing the poisonous agency of the ego: "As long as one has a body, one cannot renounce action altogether. True renunciation is giving up all desire for personal reward" (18:11). Eckhart explains,

> To be right, a person must do one of two things: either he must learn to have God in his work and hold fast to him there, or he must give up his work altogether. Since, however, man cannot live without activities that are both human and various, we must learn to keep God in everything we do, and whatever the job or place, keep on with him, letting nothing stand in our way.

It would be difficult to find a better summary of the Gita's message anywhere—and this, incidentally, from a man considered to represent the path of knowledge.

Krishna wraps all this up in one famous verse: "Abandon all supports and look to me for protection. I shall purify you of the sins of the past; do not grieve" (18:66). Krishna is the Self; the words mean simply to cast aside external props and dependencies and rely on the Self alone, seeking strength nowhere but within.

Why does selfless action lead to Self-realization? It is not a matter of "good" action being divinely rewarded. Self-realization is not some kind of compensation for good deeds. We can understand the dynamics if we remember that the Gita's emphasis is on the mind. Most human activity, good and bad, is tainted by ego-involvement. Such activity cannot purify conscious-ness, because it goes on generating new karma in the mind—in practical terms, we go on getting entangled in what we do. Selfless work purifies consciousness be-cause when there is no trace of ego involvement, new karma is not produced; the mind is simply working out the karma it has already accumulated—colloquially, its hangups.

Shankara illustrates this with the simile of a potter's wheel. The ego's job is to go on incessantly spinning the wheel of the mind and making karma-pots: new ideas to act on, fresh desires to pursue. When this pointless activity stops, no more pots are made, but for a while the wheel of the mind goes on spinning out of the momentum of its past karma. This is an anguishing period in the life of every mystic: you have done every-thing you can; now you can only wait with a kind of impatient patience. Eventually, for no reason that one can understand, the wheel does come to a stop, dissolv-ing the mind-process in samadhi.

A HIGHER IMAGE

Perhaps the clearest way to grasp the Gita is to look at the way it describes those who embody its teachings. There are portraits like this at the beginning of the Gita, the middle, and the end, each offering a model of our full human potential.

The first is given at the end of Chapter 2 (2:54–72), verses which Gandhi said hold the key to the entire Gita. Arjuna has just been told about Self-knowledge; now he asks a very practical question: when a person attains this knowledge, how does it show? How do such people conduct themselves in everyday life? We expect a list of virtues. Instead, Krishna delivers a surprise: the surest sign is that they have banished all selfish desires. Their senses and mind are completely trained, so they are free from sensory cravings and self-will. Identified completely with the Self, not with body or mind, they realize their immortality here on earth.

The implications of this are not spelled out; we have to see them in a living person. G. K. Chesterton once said that to understand the Sermon on the Mount, we should look not at Christ but at St. Francis. To understand the Gita I went to look at Mahatma Gandhi, who had done his best for forty years to translate those verses into his daily life. Seeing him, I understood that those "who see themselves in all and all in them" would simply not be capable of harming others. Augustine says daringly, "Love, then do as you like": nothing will come out of you but goodness. I saw too what it meant to view one's body with detachment: not indifference, but compassionate care as an instrument of service. I saw what it means to rest in the midst of intense action. Most important, I grasped one of the most refreshing ideas in Hindu mysticism: original goodness. Since the Self is the core of every personality, no one needs to acquire goodness or compassion; they are already there. All that is necessary is to remove the selfish habits that hide them.

Chapter 12 gives another portrait in its closing verses (12:13–20), and here we do get an inspiring list of the marks of those who follow the path of love:

> That one I love who is incapable of ill will, who is
> friendly and compassionate. Living beyond the reach of
> *I* and *mine* and of pleasure and pain, patient, contented,
> self-controlled, firm in faith, with all his heart and all
> his mind given to me—such a one is dear to me. . . .
> (12:13–14)

And finally comes the passionate description with which the Gita ends, when Krishna tells Arjuna how to recognize the man or woman who has reached life's supreme goal:

> He who is free from selfish attachments, who has mastered himself and his passions, attains the supreme perfection of freedom from action. Listen now, Arjuna, and I will describe how one who has attained perfection also attains Brahman, the supreme consummation of wisdom. . . . (18:49–50)

These are not separate paths, separate ideals. All three passages describe one person: vital, active, compassionate, self-reliant in the highest sense, for he looks to the Self for everything and needs nothing from life but the opportunity to give. In brief, such a person knows who he is, and in that knowing is everything.

This is not running away from life, as is so often claimed. It is running *into* life, open-handed, open-armed: "flying, running, and rejoicing," says Thomas a Kempis, for "he is free and will not be bound," never entangled in self-doubts, conflict, or vacillation. Far from being desireless—look at Gandhi, Catherine of Siena, St. Teresa, St. Francis—the man or woman who realizes God has yoked all human passions to the over-riding desire to give and love and serve; and in that unification we can see, not the extinction of personality, but its full blossoming. This is what it means to be fully human; our ordinary lives of stimulus and response, getting and spending, seem by comparison as faint as remembered dreams. This flowering of the spirit appeals, I think, to everyone. "This is the true joy in life," says Bernard Shaw:

> the being used for a purpose recognized by yourself as a mighty one; . . . the being a force of Nature instead of a feverish selfish little clod of ailments and grievances complaining that the world will not devote itself to making you happy.

Instead of "Nature" with a capital *N,* of course, the Gita would say "an instrument of the Self"; but that is the only difference. One of the most appealing features of the Gita for our times is that it clears up misunderstandings about the spiritual life and shows it for what it is: active, joyful, intentional, a middle path between extremes that transfigures everyday living.

FAITH AND SPIRITUAL EVOLUTION

One last untranslatable concept and I will let the Gita speak for itself. That concept is *shraddha,* and its nearest English equivalent is faith. I have translated it as such, but *shraddha* means much more. It is literally "that which is placed in the heart": all the beliefs we hold so deeply that we never think to question them. It is the set of values, axioms, prejudices, and prepossessions that colors our perceptions, governs our thinking, dictates our responses, and shapes our lives, generally without our even being aware of its presence and power.

This may sound philosophical, but shraddha is not an intellectual abstraction. It is our very substance. The Gita says, "A person is what his shraddha is" (17:3). The Bible uses almost the same words: "As a man thinketh in his heart, so is he." Shraddha reflects everything that we have made ourselves and points to what we have become. But there is nothing passive about shraddha. It is full of potency, for it prompts action, conditions behavior, and determines how we see and therefore respond to the world around us.

When Norman Cousins talks about a "belief system" analogous to the body's organ systems, that is one aspect of shraddha; he is referring to the power to heal or harm that is inherent in our ideas of ourselves. One person with a serious illness believes he has a contribution to make to the world and so he recovers; another believes his life is worthless and he dies: that is the power of shraddha. Similarly, self-image is part of shrad-dha. One person believes she will succeed in life and overcomes great obstacles; another, who believes she can do nothing, may be more gifted and face fewer difficulties but accomplish very little.

Yet shraddha is not brute determination or wishful thinking. When St. John of the Cross says "We live in what we love," he is explaining shraddha. This is our world. Our lives are an eloquent expression of our belief: what we deem worth having, doing, attaining, being. What we strive for shows what we value; we back our shraddha with our time, our energy, our very lives.

Thus shraddha determines destiny. As the Buddha puts it, "All that we are is the result of what we have thought. We are made of our thoughts; we are molded by our thoughts." As we think, so we become. This is true not only of individuals but of societies, institutions, and civilizations, according to the dominant ideas that shape their actions. To take just two examples, faith in technology is part of the shraddha of modern civilization.

"Right shraddha," according to the Gita, is faith in spiritual laws: in the unity of life, the presence of divinity in every person, the essentially spiritual nature of the human being. "Wrong shraddha" is not necessarily morally wrong, merely ignorant. It means believing that there is no more to life than physical existence, that the human being is only a biochemical entity, that happiness can be got by pursuing private interests and ignoring the rest of life. Such beliefs are misplaced: we have attached our shraddha to beliefs that life cannot bear out. Sooner or later they must prove false, and then our shraddha changes. Like our thinking, therefore—like us ourselves—shraddha evolves. The purpose of karma is to teach the consequences of shraddha, so that by trial and error, life after life, the individual soul ac-

43

quires the kind of faith that leads to fulfillment of life's
supreme goal. Krishna explains the dynamics:

> When a person is devoted to something with complete
> faith, I unify his faith in that form. Then, when his faith
> is completely unified, he gains the object of his devo-
> tion. In this way, every desire is fulfilled by me.

This is perhaps the most compassionate insight into
human evolution ever expressed. The Gita is steeped in
it, but it is not exclusive to the Gita or to Hinduism.
"Whether you like it or not, whether you know it or
not," says Meister Eckhart, "secretly Nature seeks and
hunts and tries to ferret out the track in which God may
be found." The whole purpose of every experience,
every activity, every faculty, is to turn the human being
inward and lead him back to his divine source. Thus
every person seeking satisfaction in the world outside
him—pleasure, power, profit, prestige—is really looking
for God: "As men approach me, so I receive them. All
paths, Arjuna, lead to me" (4:11).

Two forces pervade human life, the Gita says: the
upward thrust of evolution and the downward pull of
our evolutionary past. Ultimately, then, the Gita is not
a book of commandments but a book of choices. It does
mention sin, but mostly it talks about ignorance and its
consequences. Krishna tells Arjuna about the Self, the
forces of the mind, the relationship between thought
and action, the law of karma, and then concludes,
"Now, Arjuna, reflect on these words and then do as
you choose" (18:63). The struggle is between two
halves of human nature, and choices are posed every
moment. Everyone who has accepted this challenge, I
think, will testify that life offers no fiercer battle than
this war within. We have no choice about the fighting; it
is built into human nature. But we do have the choice of
which side to fight on:

44

Remembering me, you shall overcome all difficulties through my grace. But if you will not heed me in your self-will, nothing will avail you. If you egotistically say, "I will not fight this battle," your resolve will be useless; your own nature will drive you into it. (18:58–59)

Therefore, remember me at all times and fight on. With your heart and mind intent on me, you will surely come to me. (8:7)

Thus the Gita places human destiny entirely in human hands. Its world is not deterministic, but neither is it an expression of blind chance: we shape ourselves and our world by what we believe and think and act on, whether for good or for ill. In this sense the Gita opens not on Kurukshetra but on *dharmakshetra*, the field of dharma, where Arjuna and Krishna are standing for us all.

The Bhagavad Gita

Chapter One
The War Within

SRI KRISHNA consoles and instructs Prince Arjuna as he is about to go into battle against family and friends to defend his older brother's claim to the ancient throne of the Kurus. Thus the great scripture called Bhagavad Gita, the "Song of the Lord," begins. Sri Krishna is Bhagavan, "the Lord," the mysterious incarnation of Lord Vishnu, the aspect of God who fosters and preserves the universe against the forces constantly working to destroy and corrupt it. Krishna has appeared on earth as a royal prince of the house of the Yadavas; thus he combines earthly majesty with a hidden spiritual power. Ordinary men know him only as an unimportant prince, but the wise have seen him reveal his power to destroy evil and protect the good.

The battle of the Bhagavad Gita is not Krishna's fight, however; it is Arjuna's. Krishna is only Arjuna's charioteer and advisor. He has promised Arjuna that he will be with him throughout the ordeal, but much as he passionately hopes for Arjuna's victory, he has sworn to be a noncombatant in the struggle. A charioteer's position is a lowly one compared to the status and glory of the warrior he drives, but Krishna assumes this modest role out of love for Arjuna. As charioteer, he is in a perfect position to give advice and encouragement to Arjuna without violating his promise not to join the fight himself.

To secure their claim to the throne, Arjuna and his

47

brothers must fight not an alien army but their own cousins, who have held the kingdom for many years. Tragically, the forces against them include their own uncle, the blind king Dhritarashtra, and even the revered teachers and elders who guided Arjuna and his brothers when they were young. Arjuna, of course, wants to win the throne for his brother, who is the rightful heir to the Kuru dynasty and has endured many wrongs. But he is dismayed at the prospect of fighting his own people. Thus, on the morning the great battle is to begin, he turns to Krishna, his friend and spiritual advisor, and asks him the deeper questions about life that he has never asked before. The Bhagavad Gita is Krishna's answer.

Other warriors who appear elsewhere in the drama are mentioned in this first chapter of the Gita. To Indians these are familiar figures from the legendary past, but to most Western readers they will be unknown and even unpronounceable names. Arjuna and his brothers are known as the Pandavas, "the sons of Pandu": Yudhishthira, Bhima, Arjuna, Sahadeva, and Nakula. The other side is called the Kauravas, "the sons of Kuru." This is somewhat misleading, for both sides of the royal family are Kurus by birth. But the Pandavas are now in the position of appearing to be the dissident faction, so they are called "sons of Pandu" to distinguish them from the larger family.

Pandu had once been king of the kingdom of Hastinapura, but he retired into the forest on spiritual retreat and died young. While he was away his elder brother, Dhritarashtra, looked after things back at the capital. Dhritarashtra had been blind since birth, so he had never been named ruler, but he did share power with his brother. When Pandu died, consequently, his eldest son, Yudhishthira, should have succeeded him; but because Yudhishthira was only a boy, Dhritarashtra continued on after Pandu's death.

As time passed, however, Dhritarashtra's attachment to his own eldest son, Duryodhana, gradually overcame him. Instead of rising to royal impartiality and allowing Yudhishthira his fair claim, the old, blind king began to connive at his son's demand to succeed to the throne. Actually, the line of succession had grown convoluted over several generations, and it was not unthinkable that Duryodhana should rule next. But Yudhishthira's outstanding qualities and Duryodhana's corruption gradually decided the issue, at least from the moral point of view. For Duryodhana, the conflict could be resolved only on the battlefield.

Other warriors are mentioned briefly in Chapter 1. Two particularly important figures in the Mahabharata story are Drona and Bhishma. Drona was born a brahmin, a member of the priestly caste, but in search of wealth he took up the way of the warrior and excelled in the knowledge of arms. He was the teacher, the guru, of all the royal princes in their youth, the sons of Pandu and the sons of Dhritarashtra alike. Thus it was he who taught both sides the skills of war—an irony which sharp-tongued Duryodhana points out in verse 3. Arjuna, incidentally, was Drona's best pupil when it came to the bow, excelling even Drona's own son, Ashvatthama.

Bhishma, "the grandsire" of both sides, is not actually the princes' grandfather but a respected elder statesman. As Dhritarashtra's advisor of many years' standing, he considers it his duty to stand by his king and try to protect him from his weaknesses and wrong decisions.

Another figure introduced in Chapter 1 is Sanjaya, who narrates the entire Gita to the blind king Dhritarashtra. Sanjaya is not present on the battlefield, but the text tells us that the sage Vyasa, the composer of the Gita, has given him divine sight so that he can see and report everything that goes on.

Chapter 1 leaves us acutely aware that we are on a battlefield, waiting for a catastrophic war to begin; but once Krishna begins his instruction, we leave the battlefield behind and enter the realms of philosophy and mystical vision. The first chapter is but a bridge to the real subjects of the Gita, and thus need not detain us too long in our study of the poem.

Yet the first chapter has caused a great deal of debate, largely because of what it has to say about the morality of war. Basically there have been two points of view, which are almost (but perhaps not completely) irreconcilable. First, there is the orthodox Hindu viewpoint that the Gita condones war for the warrior class: it is the *dharma,* the moral duty, of soldiers to fight in a good cause, though never for evil leaders. (It should be added that this is part of an elaborate and highly chivalrous code prescribing the just rules of war.) According to this orthodox view, the lesson of the Mahabharata (and therefore of the Gita) is that although war is evil, it is an evil that cannot be avoided—an evil both tragic and honorable for the warrior himself. War in a just cause, justly waged, is also in accord with the divine will. Because of this, in the Mahabharata, Yudhishthira and his noble brothers find their peace in the next world when they have finished their duty on earth.

The mystics' point of view is more subtle. For them the battle is an allegory, a cosmic struggle between good and evil. Krishna has revealed himself on earth to re-establish spiritual well-being, and he is asking Arjuna to engage in a spiritual struggle, not a worldly one. According to this interpretation, Arjuna is asked not to fight his kith and kin but his own lower self. Mahatma Gandhi, who based his daily life on the Gita from his twenties on, felt it would be impossible to live the kind of life taught in the Gita and still engage in violence. To argue that the Gita condones violence, he said, was to give importance only to its opening verses—its preface, so to speak—and ignore the scripture itself.

For some, it helps clarify this question to look upon the Gita as an Upanishad, a mystical statement from the Vedas, that was incorporated into the warrior epic of a later age. Chapter 1 of the Gita then forms a rather perilous bridge between the warrior's world and the really important part of the Gita—Sri Krishna's revelations of spiritual truth.

1 : The War Within

DHRITARASHTRA:

1 O Sanjaya, tell me what happened at Kurukshetra, the field of dharma, where my family
and the Pandavas gathered to fight.

SANJAYA:

2 Having surveyed the forces of the Pandavas
arrayed for battle, prince Duryodhana
approached his teacher, Drona, and spoke.

3 "O my teacher, look at this mighty army of
the Pandavas, assembled by your own gifted dis-

4 ciple, Yudhishthira. There are heroic warriors
and great archers who are the equals of Bhima
and Arjuna: Yuyudhana, Virata, the mighty

5 Drupada, Dhrishtaketu, Chekitana, the
valiant king of Kashi, Purujit, Kuntibhoja,

6 the great leader Shaibya, the powerful Yudha-
manyu, the valiant Uttamaujas, and the son of
Subhadra, in addition to the sons of Draupadi.
All these command mighty chariots.

7 "O best of brahmins, listen to the names of
those who are distinguished among our own

8 forces: Bhishma, Karna, and the victorious
Kripa; Ashvatthama, Vikarna, and the son

9 of Somadatta. There are many others, too,

heroes giving up their lives for my sake, all
proficient in war and armed with a variety of
10   weapons. Our army is unlimited and commanded by Bhishma; theirs is small and com-
11   manded by Bhima. Let everyone take his
proper place and stand firm supporting
Bhishma!"

12   Then the powerful Bhishma, the grandsire,
oldest of all the Kurus, in order to cheer
Duryodhana, roared like a lion and blew his
13   conch horn. And after Bhishma, a tremen-
dous noise arose of conchs and cowhorns
and pounding on drums.

14   Then Sri Krishna and Arjuna, who were
standing in a mighty chariot yoked with
15   white horses, blew their divine conchs. Sri
Krishna blew the conch named Panchajanya,
and Arjuna blew that called Devadatta. The
mighty Bhima blew the huge conch Paundra.
16   Yudhishthira, the king, the son of Kunti,
blew the conch Anantavijaya; Nakula and
17   Sahadeva blew their conchs as well. Then the
king of Kashi, the leading bowman, the great
warrior Shikhandi, Dhrishtadyumna, Virata,
18   the invincible Satyaki, Drupada, all the sons
of Draupadi, and the strong-armed son of
19   Subhadra joined in, and the noise tore
through the heart of Duryodhana's army.
Indeed, the sound was tumultuous, echoing
throughout heaven and earth.

20   Then, O Dhritarashtra, lord of the earth,

having seen your son's forces set in their places and the fighting about to begin, Arjuna spoke these words to Sri Krishna:

ARJUNA:

21 O Krishna, drive my chariot between the
22 two armies. I want to see those who desire to fight with me. With whom will this battle be
23 fought? I want to see those assembled to fight for Duryodhana, those who seek to please the evil-minded son of Dhritarashtra by engaging in war.

SANJAYA:

24 Thus Arjuna spoke, and Sri Krishna, driving his splendid chariot between the two armies,
25 facing Bhishma and Drona and all the kings of the earth, said: "Arjuna, behold all the Kurus gathered together."

26 And Arjuna, standing between the two armies, saw fathers and grandfathers, teachers, uncles, and brothers, sons and
27 grandsons, in-laws and friends. Seeing his kinsmen established in opposition, Arjuna was overcome by sorrow. Despairing, he spoke these words:

ARJUNA:

28 O Krishna, I see my own relations here anx-
29 ious to fight, and my limbs grow weak; my mouth is dry, my body shakes, and my hair is
30 standing on end. My skin burns, and the bow Gandiva has slipped from my hand. I am un-

able to stand; my mind seems to be whirling.

31 These signs bode evil for us. I do not see that any good can come from killing our relations

32 in battle. O Krishna, I have no desire for victory, or for a kingdom or pleasures. Of what

33 use is a kingdom or pleasure or even life, if those for whose sake we desire these things—

34 teachers, fathers, sons, grandfathers, uncles, in-laws, grandsons, and others with family ties—are engaging in this battle, renouncing

35 their wealth and their lives? Even if they were to kill me, I would not want to kill them, not even to become ruler of the three worlds. How much less for the earth alone?

36 O Krishna, what satisfaction could we find in killing Dhritarashtra's sons? We would become sinners by slaying these men, even

37 though they are evil. The sons of Dhritarashtra are related to us; therefore, we should not kill them. How can we gain happiness by killing members of our own family?

38 Though they are overpowered by greed and see no evil in destroying families or injuring

39 friends, *we* see these evils. Why shouldn't we

40 turn away from this sin? When a family declines, ancient traditions are destroyed. With them are lost the spiritual foundations for life,

41 and the family loses its sense of unity. Where there is no sense of unity, the women of the family become corrupt; and with the corruption of its women, society is plunged into

42 chaos. Social chaos is hell for the family and

for those who have destroyed the family as
well. It disrupts the process of spiritual evolu-
43 tion begun by our ancestors. The timeless
spiritual foundations of family and society
would be destroyed by these terrible deeds,
which violate the unity of life.

44 It is said that those whose family dharma has
45 been destroyed dwell in hell. This is a great
sin! We are prepared to kill our own relations
out of greed for the pleasures of a kingdom.
46 Better for me if the sons of Dhritarashtra,
weapons in hand, were to attack me in battle
and kill me unarmed and unresisting.

SANJAYA:

47 Overwhelmed by sorrow, Arjuna spoke these
words. And casting away his bow and his
arrows, he sat down in his chariot in the middle of the battlefield.

Chapter Two
The Illumined Man

As ARJUNA's spiritual teacher, Sri Krishna's task now is to rouse Arjuna from his despair and set him on the way to salvation.

Arjuna is essentially a man of action, renowned for his bravery, nobility, and skill in the arts of war—intelligent, but not much given to reflection. In his present crisis, however, he finds that the active life is not enough. He is forced to ask the perennial questions about life and death: Does he have a soul? Does it survive death? Is there a deeper reality than we perceive in the world around us? If so, is it possible to know it directly, and (for Arjuna is always practical) what effect does such knowing have in everyday life?

In his answer, Krishna touches on almost all the main themes and concepts of the Gita. Chapter 2 is thus a kind of overview of the sixteen chapters to come.

Sri Krishna begins by reminding Arjuna of his immortal nature: his real Self, the Atman, never dies, for it is never born; it is eternal. Thus the Gita does not lead us from stage to stage of spiritual awareness, but begins with the ultimate premise: the immortal soul is more important than the passing world. This central mystical truth is still far from Arjuna's grasp, but for the time being he is willing to go along with what Krishna is telling him.

Knowing he is out of his depth in these inner realms

of the mind and spirit, Arjuna formally asks Krishna to be his spiritual teacher or *guru*. This is a basic pre-requisite of a disciple's initiation in the ancient Hindu tradition, where it is believed that virtually all seekers need the guidance of an experienced teacher. Arjuna is no exception, and he is fortunate to have Krishna himself as his guru. In the allegorical sense, of course, Krishna is a symbol of the Atman, Arjuna's deepest self.

This chapter introduces the idea of rebirth or *samsara*. The Self wears the body as a garment; when the garment is old, it is cast aside and a new one is put on. Thus the soul, or *jiva*, travels from life to life. Just as death is certain for the living, rebirth is certain for the dead. Krishna assures Arjuna that his basic nature is not subject to time and death; yet he reminds him that he cannot realize this truth if he cannot see beyond the dualities of life: pleasure and pain, success and failure, even heat and cold. The Gita does not teach a spirituality aimed at an enjoyable life in the hereafter, nor does it teach a way to enhance power in this life or the next. It teaches a basic detachment from pleasure and pain, as this chapter says more than once. Only in this way can an individual rise above the conditioning of life's dualities and identify with the Atman, the immortal Self.

Also, the Gita does not teach an enlightenment based on mere knowledge of the scriptures. The important thing is direct mystical experience, which Krishna will later urge Arjuna to acquire for himself.

This chapter introduces various definitions of *yoga* taught in the Gita. Here the word does not refer to the physical postures and exercises (*hatha yoga*) it connotes in the West; it refers primarily to disciplining the mind. "Yoga is evenness of mind": detachment from the dualities of pain and pleasure, success and failure, and so on. Therefore "yoga is skill in action," because this kind of detachment is required if one is to act in freedom, rather than merely react to events according to his conditioning. Krishna is not trying to get Arjuna to lead a different kind of life and renounce the world as would a monk or recluse. He tells Arjuna that if he can establish himself in yoga—in unshakable equanimity, profound peace of mind—he will be more effective in the realm of action. His judgment will be better and his vision clear if he is not emotionally entangled in the outcome of what he does.

Arjuna now asks his first question as Krishna's student. His teacher has been talking about spiritual wisdom: direct, experiential knowledge of the immortal Self. Arjuna wants to know what difference this kind of wisdom makes in everyday life. If a person has managed to establish an ever-present awareness of the core of divinity within himself, how does it affect the way he lives? Arjuna is not interested just in what such a person believes, but in how he conducts himself in life.

Krishna's answer (2:55–72) is one of the most important and most quoted passages in the Gita. Mahatma Gandhi said these verses contain the essence of the Gita: if the rest of the scripture were lost, this passage alone would be enough to teach a complete way of life. Those who are established in wisdom (*sthita-prajnas*) live in continuous, unbroken awareness that they are not the perishable body but the Atman. Further, they see the same Self in everyone, for the Atman is universally present in all.

Such a person, Krishna says, does not identify with personal desires. They are on the surface of personality, and the Self is its very core. The Self-realized man or woman is not motivated by personal desires—in other words, by any desire for *kama,* personal satisfaction. This idea is rather foreign to modern thinking, but basic to the Gita—and, indeed, to mystics of all traditions.

More specifically, the word *kama* refers to any gratification of the ego or the senses. This is not from puritan principles; it is just that sense-pleasure entangles us in the world of the senses, with all its ups and downs, and thus draws us away from the core of our being, the Self. Those established in Self-realization control their senses instead of letting their senses control them. If the senses are not controlled, Krishna warns, the mind (or emotions) will follow wherever they lead—after immediate pleasure, which is generally at odds with long-term benefit. Eventually a person following his senses loses strength of will and unity of purpose; his choices are dictated by his desires. When the will is led astray by the desire for pleasure, the mind becomes confused and scattered. Ultimately, Krishna warns, this leads to spiritual destruction:

> When you keep thinking about sense objects, attachment comes. Attachment breeds desire, the lust of possession that burns to anger. Anger clouds the judgment; you can no longer learn from past mistakes. Lost is the power to choose between the wise and the unwise, and your life is utter waste. (2:62–63)

Yet the Gita does not recommend asceticism. It is more a matter of self-control, a training of the body, mind, and senses.

At the very close of the chapter, Krishna introduces the idea that it is not enough to master all desires; it is also necessary to subdue possessiveness and ego-centricity. If this ultimate bourne can be passed, then the seeker will know the true, immortal Self within. This is the mystics' ultimate goal: knowing their real nature, they know their own immortality and realize their union with eternal Being.

2 : *The Illumined Man*

SANJAYA:

SANJAYA:

1 These are the words that Sri Krishna spoke to
the despairing Arjuna, whose eyes were burning with tears of pity and confusion.

SRI KRISHNA:

2 This despair and weakness in a time of crisis
are mean and unworthy of you, Arjuna. How
have you fallen into a state so far from the
3 path to liberation? It does not become you to
yield to this weakness. Arise with a brave
heart and destroy the enemy.

ARJUNA:

4 How can I ever bring myself to fight against
Bhishma and Drona, who are worthy of rev-
5 erence? How can I, Krishna? Surely it would
be better to spend my life begging than to kill
these great and worthy souls! If I killed them,
every pleasure I found would be tainted. I
6 don't even know which would be better, for
us to conquer them or for them to conquer us.
The sons of Dhritarashtra have confronted us;
but why would we care to live if we killed
them?

7   My will is paralyzed, and I am utterly confused. Tell me which is the better path for me.
Let me be your disciple. I have fallen at your

8   feet; give me instruction. What can overcome
a sorrow that saps all my vitality? Even power
over men and gods or the wealth of an empire
seems empty.

SANJAYA:

9   This is how Arjuna, the great warrior, spoke
to Sri Krishna. With the words, "O Krishna, I
will not fight," he fell silent.

10   As they stood between the two armies, Sri
Krishna smiled and replied to Arjuna, who
had sunk into despair.

SRI KRISHNA:

11   You speak sincerely, but your sorrow has no
cause. The wise grieve neither for the living

12   nor for the dead. There has never been a time
when you and I and the kings gathered here
have not existed, nor will there be a time

13   when we will cease to exist. As the same
person inhabits the body through childhood,
youth, and old age, so too at the time of death
he attains another body. The wise are not
deluded by these changes.

14   When the senses contact sense objects, a
person experiences cold or heat, pleasure or
pain. These experiences are fleeting; they
come and go. Bear them patiently, Arjuna.

15   Those who are not affected by these changes,

who are the same in pleasure and pain, are
truly wise and fit for immortality. Assert your
strength and realize this!

16   The impermanent has no reality; reality
lies in the eternal. Those who have seen the
boundary between these two have attained the
17   end of all knowledge. Realize that which pervades the universe and is indestructible; no
power can affect this unchanging, imperish-
18   able reality. The body is mortal, but he who
dwells in the body is immortal and immeasurable. Therefore, Arjuna, fight in this battle.

19   One man believes he is the slayer, another
believes he is the slain. Both are ignorant;
20   there is neither slayer nor slain. You were
never born; you will never die. You have
never changed; you can never change.
Unborn, eternal, immutable, immemorial,
21   you do not die when the body dies. Realizing
that which is indestructible, eternal, unborn,
and unchanging, how can you slay or cause
another to slay?

22   As a man abandons worn-out clothes and
acquires new ones, so when the body is
worn out a new one is acquired by the Self,
who lives within.

23   The Self cannot be pierced by weapons or
burned by fire; water cannot wet it, nor can
24   the wind dry it. The Self cannot be pierced or
burned, made wet or dry. It is everlasting and

infinite, standing on the motionless founda-
25 tions of eternity. The Self is unmanifested,
beyond all thought, beyond all change.
Knowing this, you should not grieve.

26 O mighty Arjuna, even if you believe the Self
to be subject to birth and death, you should
27 not grieve. Death is inevitable for the living;
birth is inevitable for the dead. Since these are
28 unavoidable, you should not sorrow. Every
creature is unmanifested at first and then
attains manifestation. When its end has come,
it once again becomes unmanifested. What is
there to lament in this?

29 The glory of the Self is beheld by a few, and
a few describe it; a few listen, but many with-
30 out understanding. The Self of all beings,
living within the body, is eternal and cannot
be harmed. Therefore, do not grieve.

31 Considering your dharma, you should not
vacillate. For a warrior, nothing is higher than
32 a war against evil. The warrior confronted
with such a war should be pleased, Arjuna,
33 for it comes as an open gate to heaven. But if
you do not participate in this battle against
evil, you will incur sin, violating your dharma
and your honor.

34 The story of your dishonor will be repeated
endlessly: and for a man of honor, dishonor is
35 worse than death. These brave warriors will
think you have withdrawn from battle out of

fear, and those who formerly esteemed you
36 will treat you with disrespect. Your enemies
will ridicule your strength and say things that
should not be said. What could be more painful than this?

37 Death means the attainment of heaven; victory
means the enjoyment of the earth. Therefore
38 rise up, Arjuna, resolved to fight! Having
made yourself alike in pain and pleasure,
profit and loss, victory and defeat, engage in
this great battle and you will be freed from
sin.

39 You have heard the intellectual explanation of
Sankhya, Arjuna; now listen to the principles
of yoga. By practicing these you can break
40 through the bonds of karma. On this path
effort never goes to waste, and there is no
failure. Even a little effort toward spiritual
awareness will protect you from the greatest
fear.

41 Those who follow this path, resolving deep
within themselves to seek Me alone, attain
singleness of purpose. For those who lack
resolution, the decisions of life are many-
branched and endless.

42 There are ignorant people who speak flowery
words and take delight in the letter of the law,
43 saying that there is nothing else. Their hearts
are full of selfish desires, Arjuna. Their idea of
heaven is their own enjoyment, and the aim of

all their activities is pleasure and power. The
fruit of their actions is continual rebirth.

44 Those whose minds are swept away by the
pursuit of pleasure and power are incapable of
following the supreme goal and will not attain
samadhi.

45 The scriptures describe the three gunas. But
you should be free from the action of the
gunas, established in eternal truth, self-
controlled, without any sense of duality or
the desire to acquire and hoard.

46 Just as a reservoir is of little use when the
whole countryside is flooded, scriptures are of
little use to the illumined man or woman,
who sees the Lord everywhere.

47 You have the right to work, but never to
the fruit of work. You should never engage
in action for the sake of reward, nor should
48 you long for inaction. Perform work in this
world, Arjuna, as a man established within
himself—without selfish attachments, and
alike in success and defeat. For yoga is perfect
evenness of mind.

49 Seek refuge in the attitude of detachment and
you will amass the wealth of spiritual awareness. Those who are motivated only by desire
for the fruits of action are miserable, for they
are constantly anxious about the results of
50 what they do. When consciousness is unified,
however, all vain anxiety is left behind. There

is no cause for worry, whether things go well or ill. Therefore, devote yourself to the disciplines of yoga, for yoga is skill in action.

51 The wise unify their consciousness and abandon attachment to the fruits of action, which binds a person to continual rebirth. Thus they attain a state beyond all evil.

52 When your mind has overcome the confusion of duality, you will attain the state of holy indifference to things you hear and things you
53 have heard. When you are unmoved by the confusion of ideas and your mind is completely united in deep samadhi, you will attain the state of perfect yoga.

ARJUNA:

54 Tell me of those who live established in wisdom, ever aware of the Self, O Krishna. How do they talk? How sit? How move about?

SRI KRISHNA:

55 They live in wisdom who see themselves in all and all in them, who have renounced every selfish desire and sense craving tormenting the heart.

56 Neither agitated by grief nor hankering after pleasure, they live free from lust and fear and anger. Established in meditation, they are
57 truly wise. Fettered no more by selfish attachments, they are neither elated by good fortune nor depressed by bad. Such are the seers.

58 Even as a tortoise draws in its limbs, the wise
59 can draw in their senses at will. Aspirants abstain from sense pleasures, but they still crave
for them. These cravings all disappear when
60 they see the highest goal. Even of those who
tread the path, the stormy senses can sweep
61 off the mind. They live in wisdom who
subdue their senses and keep their minds ever
absorbed in me.

62 When you keep thinking about sense objects,
attachment comes. Attachment breeds desire,
63 the lust of possession that burns to anger. Anger clouds the judgment; you can no longer
learn from past mistakes. Lost is the power to
choose between what is wise and what is un-
64 wise, and your life is utter waste. But when
you move amidst the world of sense, free
65 from attachment and aversion alike, there
comes the peace in which all sorrows end,
and you live in the wisdom of the Self.

66 The disunited mind is far from wise; how
can it meditate? How be at peace? When you
know no peace, how can you know joy?
67 When you let your mind follow the call of the
senses, they carry away your better judgment
as storms drive a boat off its charted course on
the sea.

68 Use all your power to free the senses from
attachment and aversion alike, and live in the
69 full wisdom of the Self. Such a sage awakes to
light in the night of all creatures. That which

the world calls day is the night of ignorance to
the wise.

70 As rivers flow into the ocean but cannot make
the vast ocean overflow, so flow the streams
of the sense-world into the sea of peace that is
the sage. But this is not so with the desirer of
desires.

71 They are forever free who renounce all selfish
desires and break away from the ego-cage of
"I," "me," and "mine" to be united with the
72 Lord. This is the supreme state. Attain to this,
and pass from death to immortality.

Chapter Three
Selfless Service

THE TITLE of this chapter in Sanskrit is Karma Yoga, "The Way of Action," and here we take an apparently sharp turn away from the subject of the previous chapter. In fact, Arjuna changes the subject completely. Krishna has been trying to convince him that he has an immortal soul, but Arjuna continues to worry about his immediate predicament. It is not that he is uninterested in mystical enlightenment, but his main concern at the moment is just what he is supposed to do next.

Or, he asks, perhaps what he does is not so important after all. Has Krishna been telling him to concentrate on acquiring spiritual wisdom and to forget about his apparent duties in the world?

Krishna replies that there is no way Arjuna can avoid the obligation of selfless action, or karma yoga. Arjuna must act selflessly, out of a sense of duty. He must work not for his own sake, but for the welfare of all. Krishna points out that this is a basic law underlying all creation. Each being must do its part in the grand scheme of things, and there is no way to avoid this obligation—except perhaps by the complete enlightenment which loosens all the old bonds of karma.

Here the Gita refers to the doctrine of karma, which is one of the most basic teachings in the Hindu and Buddhist scriptures. *Karma* literally means deed or action; what is sometimes called the "law of karma" refers to an underlying law of cause and effect that is seen to permeate all existence. The idea is that every action leads to a reasonable result—and, consequently, that everything that happens can be traced to something done in the past. Actions determine destiny: this is the basic idea of karma. If anything happens to us that is truly good, we must have done something in the past to deserve it; if something ill befalls us, then at some time in the past we did something that was not so meritorious. This is a basic moral law that all great spiritual traditions share. It is a belief that we reap what we sow.

The Hindu tradition gave a great deal of thought to this problem of moral cause and effect, and generation after generation of spiritual teachers fathomed its depths and implications. One fear that developed over time was that all action was in a sense an open door to bondage: anything a person did would bind him to the endless cycle of cause and effect. Some "fruits" of action would of course be pleasant—not all karma is painful. But even this pleasure could be a trap, because we would seek it compulsively, tying ourselves tighter and tighter to the responsibilities and opportunities of the worldly life and forgetting our spiritual dimension altogether.

In Chapter 3 Krishna begins to tell Arjuna the way out of this maze of cause and effect. It is not to avoid work, especially the duties required by his station in life, but to perform those duties without selfish attachment to their "fruit," or outcome. If Arjuna follows this path of selfless work, Krishna explains, he will enjoy this world as well as the next. More important, he will gain a spiritual blessing and will be lessening his debt of karma. Only when he is free from every bond of karma—every consequence of past action—can he achieve life's ultimate goal.

The world is bound in its own activity, for all creatures except the illumined man or woman work for their own pleasure and gain. Because they act selfishly, they are bound by the results, whether good or bad. We must act in a selfless spirit, Krishna says, without ego-involvement and without getting entangled in whether things work out the way we want; only then will we not fall into the terrible net of karma. We cannot hope to escape karma by refraining from our duties: even to survive in the world, we must act out our role.

True, the Hindu scriptures do hold out another path—*jnana yoga,* the path of wisdom—which does not enjoin action. But Krishna does not really offer this to Arjuna as an alternative; it is simply mentioned and then dropped. Perhaps Krishna knows that Arjuna is not the type to disengage himself and go off on a search for the mystical vision, or perhaps Krishna does not really approve of the path of knowledge. In any case he doesn't instruct Arjuna in that direction. For Arjuna, the active life is essential.

The danger, of course, of a life of active engagement in the world is that Arjuna will get caught up in his actions and begin to act out of selfish motives. If this were to happen, he would be doomed to spiritual failure.

Having a good deal of self-knowledge, Arjuna senses this danger. He asks Krishna a fundamental question: What power binds us to our selfish ways? Even if we wish to act rightly, so often we do the wrong thing. What power moves us?

Krishna replies that anger and selfish desire are our greatest enemies. They are the destructive powers that can compel us to wander away from our purpose, to end up in self-delusion and despair.

Here it is necessary to introduce two technical terms from Hindu philosophy. The Gita is not an academic work of philosophy, but a poetic, practical work for a

73

lay audience. Still, it does refer from time to time to Sankhya, one of the six traditional schools of Indian philosophy. In Sankhya, the phenomenal world of mind and matter is described as having three basic qualities or *gunas*: *sattva*—goodness, light, purity; *rajas*—passion, activity, energy; and *tamas*—darkness, ignorance, inertia. According to Sankhya, spiritual evolution progresses from tamas to rajas to sattva, and final liberation takes the soul beyond the three gunas altogether.

Here Krishna warns Arjuna to beware the pitfalls of rajas, for it is from rajas that anger and selfish desire arise. Arjuna must realize that his true nature, the Atman, is above entanglement in the gunas. The gunas act and react upon one another, but Arjuna's inner being is not affected. If he cannot reach this detachment, he will be always caught in the emotional storms of passion (rajas) or the quagmires of inertia (tamas) which commonly alternate in dominating the mind and body.

Krishna offers Arjuna the example of King Janaka, well known from holy legend, as a model for the princely estate. Janaka was a king who ruled well and did not shirk his responsibilities, yet he was detached and worked from a sense of duty, not for personal gain or enjoyment. He was revered as a royal sage who pursued his enlightenment not by renouncing the world, but by working in it to the best of his ability and contributing to its welfare, thus enjoying the best of both worlds.

3 : Selfless Service

1 O Krishna, you have said that knowledge is
greater than action; why then do you ask me
2 to wage this terrible war? Your advice seems
inconsistent. Give me one path to follow to
the supreme good.

SRI KRISHNA:

3 At the beginning of time I declared two paths
for the pure heart: *jnana yoga,* the contemplative path of spiritual wisdom, and *karma yoga,*
the active path of selfless service.

4 He who shirks action does not attain freedom; no one can gain perfection by abstain-
5 ing from work. Indeed, there is no one who
rests for even an instant; every creature is
driven to action by his own nature.

6 Those who abstain from action while allowing the mind to dwell on sensual pleasure can-
7 not be called sincere spiritual aspirants. But
they excel who control their senses through
the mind, using them for selfless service.

8 Fulfill all your duties; action is better than

inaction. Even to maintain your body,

9 Arjuna, you are obliged to act. Selfish action imprisons the world. Act selflessly, without any thought of personal profit.

10 At the beginning, mankind and the obligation of selfless service were created together. "Through selfless service, you will always be fruitful and find the fulfillment of your desires": this is the promise of the Creator.

11 Honor and cherish the devas as they honor and cherish you; through this honor and love

12 you will attain the supreme good. All human desires are fulfilled by the devas, who are pleased by selfless service. But anyone who enjoys the things given by the devas without offering selfless acts in return is a thief.

13 The spiritually minded, who eat in the spirit of service, are freed from all their sins; but the selfish, who prepare food for their own satis-

14 faction, eat sin. Living creatures are nourished by food, and food is nourished by rain; rain itself is the water of life, which comes from selfless worship and service.

15 Every selfless act, Arjuna, is born from Brahman, the eternal, infinite Godhead. He is

16 present in every act of service. All life turns on this law, O Arjuna. Whoever violates it, indulging his senses for his own pleasure and ignoring the needs of others, has wasted his

17 life. But those who realize the Self are always

satisfied. Having found the source of joy and
fulfillment, they no longer seek happiness

18 from the external world. They have nothing
to gain or lose by any action; neither people
nor things can affect their security.

19 Strive constantly to serve the welfare of
the world; by devotion to selfless work one
20 attains the supreme goal of life. Do your
work with the welfare of others always in
mind. It was by such work that Janaka
attained perfection; others, too, have
followed this path.

21 What the outstanding person does, others
will try to do. The standards such people
create will be followed by the whole world.
22 There is nothing in the three worlds for me to
gain, Arjuna, nor is there anything I do not
have; I continue to act, but I am not driven
23 by any need of my own. If I ever refrained
from continuous work, everyone would im-
24 mediately follow my example. If I stopped
working I would be the cause of cosmic
chaos, and finally of the destruction of this
world and these people.

25 The ignorant work for their own profit,
Arjuna; the wise work for the welfare of the
26 world, without thought for themselves. By
abstaining from work you will confuse the
ignorant, who are engrossed in their actions.
Perform all work carefully, guided by compassion.

27 All actions are performed by the gunas of
   prakriti. Deluded by his identification with
28 the ego, a person thinks, "*I* am the doer." But
   the illumined man or woman understands the
   domain of the gunas and is not attached. Such
   people know that the gunas interact with each
   other; they do not claim to be the doer.

29 Those who are deluded by the operation of
   the gunas become attached to the results of
   their action. Those who understand these
30 truths should not unsettle the ignorant. Performing all actions for my sake, completely
   absorbed in the Self, and without expectations, fight!—but stay free from the fever of
   the ego.

31 Those who live in accordance with these
   divine laws without complaining, firmly
   established in faith, are released from karma.
32 Those who violate these laws, criticizing and
   complaining, are utterly deluded, and are the
   cause of their own suffering.

33 Even a wise man acts within the limitations of
   his own nature. Every creature is subject to
34 prakriti; what is the use of repression? The
   senses have been conditioned by attraction to
   the pleasant and aversion to the unpleasant.
   Do not be ruled by them; they are obstacles in
   your path.

35 It is better to strive in one's own dharma than
   to succeed in the dharma of another. Nothing

is ever lost in following one's own dharma, but competition in another's dharma breeds fear and insecurity.

ARJUNA:

36 What is the force that binds us to selfish deeds, O Krishna? What power moves us, even against our will, as if forcing us?

SRI KRISHNA:

37 It is selfish desire and anger, arising from the guna of rajas; these are the appetites and evils which threaten a person in this life.

38 Just as a fire is covered by smoke and a mirror is obscured by dust, just as the embryo rests deep within the womb, knowledge is hidden

39 by selfish desire—hidden, Arjuna, by this unquenchable fire for self-satisfaction, the inveterate enemy of the wise. that which overcomes) our awareness

40 Selfish desire is found in the senses, mind, and intellect, misleading them and burying

41 the understanding in delusion. Fight with all your strength, Arjuna! Controlling your senses, conquer your enemy, the destroyer of knowledge and realization.

42 The senses are higher than the body, the mind higher than the senses; above the mind is the intellect, and above the intellect

43 is the Atman. Thus, knowing that which is supreme, let the Atman rule the ego. Use your mighty arms to slay the fierce enemy that is selfish desire.

79

Chapter Four
Wisdom in Action

ARJUNA IS TAKING time to grasp this profound message. Krishna is keen on granting Arjuna knowledge of the highest spiritual truths, or even a rare mystical vision; but Arjuna has been asking, more or less, for Krishna just to get him out of his present difficulties. Of course these difficulties are not minor—he is caught in a family problem that has developed into a really nasty confrontation. If he cannot extricate himself, he knows that he will have to take part in a catastrophic battle that no one really wants.

So when Krishna begins to tell Arjuna about the "secret teachings" he will be privileged to hear because he is Krishna's favorite devotee and friend, it hardly registers in Arjuna's consciousness. His only reply is hopelessly confused. "How could you have taught any secret wisdom to the sages of old?" he asks.

At this point Krishna reminds Arjuna again of the process of rebirth. They have both been reborn many times, but naturally Arjuna does not remember his past lives because he has no access to this kind of knowledge. Krishna remembers his former births, but he is no ordinary being. He reveals that he has chosen to take on human birth many times for the welfare of the world. Whenever dharma, the law of life's unity, declines, he wraps himself in his maya and takes on a finite form. Thus he returns age after age.

Vishnu, the preserving or sustaining Person of the

Hindu Trinity, is not mentioned here, but Krishna is usually looked upon as an incarnation of this particular aspect of God. As the Lord, Krishna explains, he dwells in every being, but he is manifested with special power in his incarnations or *avatars*. *Avatara* literally means descent: Vishnu is believed to descend to or incarnate himself on earth from time to time to reestablish divine law (dharma). Without such intervention the entire created universe would go into decline. The natural course of creation is to go through cycles of regeneration and decay, but Vishnu—Krishna—has a soft corner in his heart for all the suffering of the world, and comes himself to protect the good and destroy evil. Thus Vishnu has a special relationship with all beings: he personifies the aspect of God who so loves the world that he comes into it in person to reestablish the purity and happiness of the Golden Age.

Krishna here reveals a little of his hidden, divine nature. He tells Arjuna that mystical union with him is possible through devotion, by which one can enter the state of divine love in which one sees God in every creature. Krishna also takes on the role of creator. It is he who has patterned the world along the lines of guna, karma, and caste.

It is not easy to understand what this mystic aspect of Krishna's being meant to the author of the Gita. In the Mahabharata, Krishna is a princely ally who is wise and daring in his support of his friend Arjuna. But the author of the Gita is not concerned with this Krishna; he turns his attention to the mystery of Krishna's divine nature as an aspect of Vishnu. In this sense Krishna is the inner Self in all beings. His name comes from the Sanskrit root *krish,* which originally meant "to draw a plough" and thus "to draw to oneself, to attract." He is the "attractive one," the "Lord of loving attraction." By another etymology, the word *Krishna* also means "the dark one." The author of the Gita sees revealed in him the ultimate Godhead, the supreme being. But this reality is often veiled, and then Krishna is seen as an ordinary man—or, rather, as an exceptionally gifted man, but not as God.

At any rate, many of Krishna's lines make most sense as spiritual instruction when we realize that when he speaks of himself, he is often not describing a transcendental reality so much as trying to tell Arjuna about the Self in every human being. When he says, for example, "Actions do not cling to me because I am not attached to their results," he means, "Arjuna, actions do not cling to your real Self." The Self in us is not touched by action; whatever we do, it remains unsullied. "Those who understand this"—about themselves—"and practice it live in freedom."

The latter part of this chapter turns from lofty mystical topics back to Arjuna's immediate problem. Krishna begins to talk about action, and work, and things that should be done and should not be done. It is essential, he reminds Arjuna, to act wisely, with detachment. The wise never act with selfish attachment to the fruit of their labor; they give their best in fortune and misfortune alike. Such people act in freedom.

The next section deals with the various kinds of *yajna*—worship or offering—that may be performed by spiritual aspirants of differing temperaments. Ancient Hindu rituals often involved making an offering to the gods by pouring an oblation into the sacred fire. Here the image is the same: whatever is offered is symbolically thrown into a consuming fire that carries the offering to God. The offering may be as obvious as worldly goods, or as subtle as knowledge or meditation: in any case it requires a measure of self-sacrifice. Yajna is a basic action, necessary to life, and those who do not perform some kind of selfless service find no home in this world or the next.

The final verses of Chapter 4 introduce a new point.

In the last chapter, Krishna mentioned the path of spiritual wisdom as an alternative to the path of action or karma yoga. Now he reveals that wisdom is the end of selfless action: knowing is the fruit of doing. The goal of all karma yoga or yajna is liberation and spiritual wisdom. The fire of spiritual awareness burns to ashes even a great deal of karma; thus true knowledge is the greatest purifier of the soul.

Krishna ends by exhorting Arjuna to cut through the doubts that still stifle him. This is the first—but not the last—mention that Krishna makes of Arjuna's doubting heart. There has been no indication so far that Arjuna has really taken in and accepted Krishna's words. But even though Arjuna may continue to drag his feet, Krishna does not abandon him.

4 : *Wisdom in Action*

SRI KRISHNA:

1 I told this eternal secret to Vivasvat.
Vivasvat taught Manu, and Manu taught
2 Ikshvaku. Thus, Arjuna, eminent sages
received knowledge of yoga in a continuous
tradition. But through time the practice of
yoga was lost in the world.

3 The secret of these teachings is profound. I
have explained them to you today because
you are my friend and devotee.

ARJUNA:

4 You were born much after Vivasvat; he lived
very long ago. Why do you say that you
taught this yoga in the beginning?

SRI KRISHNA:

5 You and I have passed through many births,
Arjuna. You have forgotten, but I remember
them all.

6 My true being is unborn and changeless.
I am the Lord who dwells in every creature.
Through the power of my own maya, I
manifest myself in a finite form.

7 Whenever dharma declines and the purpose
of life is forgotten, I manifest myself on earth.
8 I am born in every age to protect the good,
to destroy evil, and to re-establish dharma.

9 He who knows me as his own divine Self
breaks through the belief that he is the body
and is not reborn as a separate creature. Such
10 a one, Arjuna, is united with me. Delivered
from selfish attachment, fear, and anger, filled
with me, surrendering themselves to me,
purified in the fire of my being, many have
reached the state of unity in me.

11 As men approach me, so I receive them.
All paths, Arjuna, lead to me.

12 Those desiring success in their actions worship the gods; through action in the world
of mortals, their desires are quickly fulfilled.
13 The distinctions of caste, guna, and karma
have come from me. I am their cause, but I
myself am changeless and beyond all action.
14 Actions do not cling to me because I am not
attached to their results. Those who understand this and practice it live in freedom.
15 Knowing this truth, aspirants desiring liberation in ancient times engaged in action. You
too can do the same, pursuing an active life
in the manner of those ancient sages.

16 What is action and what is inaction? This
question has confused the greatest sages. I
will give you the secret of action, with which

17 you can free yourself from bondage. The true
nature of action is difficult to grasp. You
must understand what is action and what is
inaction, and what kind of action should be
avoided.

18 The wise see that there is action in the midst
of inaction and inaction in the midst of action.
Their consciousness is unified, and every act is
done with complete awareness.

19 The awakened sages call a person wise when
all his undertakings are free from anxiety
about results; all his selfish desires have been
20 consumed in the fire of knowledge. The wise,
ever satisfied, have abandoned all external
supports. Their security is unaffected by the
results of their action; even while acting, they
21 really do nothing at all. Free from expectations and from all sense of possession, with
mind and body firmly controlled by the Self,
they do not incur sin by the performance of
physical action.

22 They live in freedom who have gone beyond
the dualities of life. Competing with no one,
they are alike in success and failure and con-
23 tent with whatever comes to them. They are
free, without selfish attachments; their minds
are fixed in knowledge. They perform all
work in the spirit of service, and their karma
is dissolved.

24 The process of offering is Brahman; that

which is offered is Brahman. Brahman offers the sacrifice in the fire of Brahman. Brahman is attained by those who see Brahman in every action.

25 Some aspirants offer material sacrifices to the gods. Others offer selfless service as sacrifice
26 in the fire of Brahman. Some renounce all enjoyment of the senses, sacrificing them in the fire of sense restraint. Others partake of sense objects but offer them in service through the
27 fire of the senses. Some offer the workings of the senses and the vital forces through the fire of self-control, kindled in the path of knowledge.

28 Some offer wealth; others offer sense restraint and suffering. Some take vows and offer knowledge and study of the scriptures; and
29 some make the offering of meditation. Some offer the forces of vitality, regulating their inhalation and exhalation, and thus gain control
30 over these forces. Others offer the forces of vitality through restraint of their senses. All these understand the meaning of service and will be cleansed of their impurities.

31 True sustenance is in service, and through it a man or woman reaches the eternal Brahman. But those who do not seek to serve are without a home in this world. Arjuna, how can they be at home in any world to come?

32 These offerings are born of work, and each

guides mankind along a path to Brahman. Understanding this, you will attain liberation.

33 The offering of wisdom is better than any material offering, Arjuna; for the goal of all work is spiritual wisdom.

34 Approach someone who has realized the purpose of life and question him with reverence and devotion; he will instruct you in this wis-
35 dom. Once you attain it, you will never again be deluded. You will see all creatures in the Self, and all in me.

36 Even if you were the most sinful of sinners, Arjuna, you could cross beyond all sin by the
37 raft of spiritual wisdom. As the heat of a fire reduces wood to ashes, the fire of knowledge
38 burns to ashes all karma. Nothing in this world purifies like spiritual wisdom. It is the perfection achieved in time through the path of yoga, the path which leads to the Self within.

39 Those who take wisdom as their highest goal, whose faith is deep and whose senses are trained, attain wisdom quickly and enter
40 into perfect peace. But the ignorant, indecisive and lacking in faith, waste their lives. They can never be happy in this world or any other.

41 Those established in the Self have renounced selfish attachments to their actions and cut through doubts with spiritual wisdom. They

42 act in freedom. Arjuna, cut through this
doubt in your own heart with the sword of
spiritual wisdom. Arise; take up the path of
yoga!

Chapter Five
Renounce & Rejoice

AT THE BEGINNING of this chapter the traditional approach to the spiritual life–that is, "leaving" the world, retiring from the ordinary affairs of job, family, and the like–is contrasted with working in the world with detachment. The general term for retiring from the world is *sannyasa,* "renunciation." Traditionally, sannyasa meant renouncing all worldly ties and attachments. The person undertaking the vow of sannyasa would leave home, family, and occupation to pursue a strict contemplative life.

Of course, this was a path chosen by relatively few, even in ancient India. Yet we shouldn't forget that surprising numbers of people in traditional societies, both in the East and the West, have chosen a monastic life removed from the turmoil of the world. In India, the Compassionate Buddha provides the classic example of the man who leaves the comforts and fulfillments of family and worldly life to seek the lonely way to Self-realization. The story is well known throughout Asia. Siddhartha Gautama was a prince with every worldly satisfaction within his reach, who left his palace to find a way to lead the world beyond suffering and death. He became a wandering sannyasi, a lonely, austere monk. Only after he had attained to complete enlightenment did he return to society, to teach others of the peace of nirvana.

Though Krishna admits here that this way of sannyasa can lead to the goal, he recommends the path of selfless action or selfless service as the better way. He contrasts the way of Sankhya—which in this context means knowledge of the Self in a general way—to the way of yoga, which here means the way of action. This term *yoga* presents difficulties in the Gita because it means different things at different times, and many definitions are given of this all-purpose term. But for several chapters the topic under discussion has been the active spiritual life or karma yoga, and that is clearly what is meant in this context. *Sankhya* and *yoga* might also be translated as "theory and practice."

It would seem that at the time of the Gita the path of wisdom was regarded very highly, while the path of action may have been looked upon as an adulteration of the spiritual life. It is even possible that the Gita was the first Hindu scripture to introduce the novel idea of combining karma yoga with the pursuit of self-knowledge. Krishna says that only immature, inexperienced people look upon the paths of knowledge and action as different. The true goal of action is knowledge of the Self. Following either path faithfully will lead to the complete spiritual vision.

But it is essential in karma yoga that the selfish ego not expect gratification from the work. When there is no selfish involvement in work, the worker does not come to spiritual harm. The example is the lotus: it spends its life floating in water, yet the drops of water roll off its leaves without ever really wetting them. Similarly, as long as the karma yogi does not expect reward or recognition, any evil that might stain him has nowhere to cling. Such a person is said to be detached from the outcome or fruits of his actions (*karma phala*).

Krishna warns Arjuna that a life of work, even successful work, cannot be fulfilling without self-knowledge. Ultimately, the true Self within him is not affected by what he does, whether good or bad. Only knowledge of the Self, which rises like the sun at dawn, can fulfill the purpose of his life and lead him beyond rebirth.

This knowledge of the Self or Atman is, by its very nature, also knowledge of Brahman, the all-pervading, immanent and transcendent Godhead. Krishna says that the illumined person sees this divine essence in all beings. He or she has "equal vision" and sees the divine Self in all, regardless of the outer aspect.

The last three verses of the chapter describe a state of profound meditation called samadhi. When meditation becomes very deep, breathing becomes slow, steady, and even, and the windows of the senses close to all outward sensations. Next the faculties of the mind quiet down, resting from their usually frantic activity; even the primal emotions of desire, fear, and anger subside. When all these sensory and emotional tides have ceased to flow, then the spirit is free, *mukta*—at least for the time being. It has entered the state called samadhi.

Samadhi can come and go; generally it can be entered only in a long period of meditation and after many years of ardent endeavor. But one verse (5:28) adds the significant word *sada,* "always." Once this state of deep concentration becomes established, the person lives in spiritual freedom, or *moksha,* permanently. This is extremely rare. Mystics of the West as well as the East have attained brief glimpses of unity, but very few can be said to have dwelt in it permanently, as if it were their natural habitat. Perhaps the most articulate examples from the West are Meister Eckhart, St. Teresa of Avila, and St. John of the Cross, though there have been others. In the Hindu tradition there is a long line of saints and mystics who have tried to communicate something of the nature of this union with Reality or God, from the unknown recorders of the Upanishads through the Buddha, Shankara, and Mira, to Ramakrishna and Ramana Maharshi in our own time—to name but a very few.

5 : Renounce & Rejoice

ARJUNA:

1   O Krishna, you have recommended both the
    path of selfless action and *sannyasa,* the path of
    renunciation of action. Tell me definitely
    which is better.

SRI KRISHNA:

2   Both renunciation of action and the selfless
    performance of action lead to the supreme
    goal. But the path of action is better than
    renunciation.

3   Those who have attained perfect renunciation
    are free from any sense of duality; they are un-
    affected by likes and dislikes, Arjuna, and are
    free from the bondage of self-will. The im-
4   mature think that knowledge and action are
    different, but the wise see them as the same.
    The person who is established in one path
5   will attain the rewards of both. The goal of
    knowledge and the goal of service are the
    same; those who fail to see this are blind.

6   Perfect renunciation is difficult to attain with-
    out performing action. But the wise, follow-
    ing the path of selfless service, quickly reach
    Brahman.

7   Those who follow the path of service, who
    have completely purified themselves and con-
    quered their senses and self-will, see the Self
    in all creatures and are untouched by any
    action they perform.

8   Those who know this truth, whose con-
    sciousness is unified, think always, "I am not
    the doer." While seeing or hearing, touching
    or smelling; eating, moving about, or sleep-
9   ing; breathing or speaking, letting go or hold-
    ing on, even opening or closing the eyes, they
    understand that these are only the movements
    of the senses among sense objects.

10 Those who surrender to Brahman all selfish
    attachments are like the leaf of a lotus floating
    clean and dry in water. Sin cannot touch
11 them. Renouncing their selfish attachments,
    those who follow the path of service work
    with body, senses, and mind for the sake of
    self-purification.

12 Those whose consciousness is unified aban-
    don all attachment to the results of action and
    attain supreme peace. But those whose desires
    are fragmented, who are selfishly attached to
    the results of their work, are bound in every-
    thing they do.

13 Those who renounce attachment in all their
    deeds live content in the "city of nine gates,"
    the body, as its master. They are not driven to
    act, nor do they involve others in action.

14 Neither the sense of acting, nor actions, nor
the connection of cause and effect comes from
the Lord of this world. These three arise from
nature.

15 The Lord does not partake in the good and
evil deeds of any person; judgment is clouded
16 when wisdom is obscured by ignorance. But
ignorance is destroyed by knowledge of the
Self within. The light of this knowledge
shines like the sun, revealing the supreme
17 Brahman. Those who cast off sin through this
knowledge, absorbed in the Lord and established in him as their one goal and refuge, are
not reborn as separate creatures.

18 Those who possess this wisdom have equal
regard for all. They see the same Self in a spiritual aspirant and an outcaste, in an elephant, a
19 cow, and a dog. Such people have mastered
life. With even mind they rest in Brahman,
who is perfect and is everywhere the same.
20 They are not elated by good fortune nor
depressed by bad. With mind established in
21 Brahman, they are free from delusion. Not
dependent on any external support, they realize the joy of spiritual awareness. With consciousness unified through meditation, they
live in abiding joy.

22 Pleasures conceived in the world of the senses
have a beginning and an end and give birth to
misery, Arjuna. The wise do not look for
23 happiness in them. But those who overcome

the impulses of lust and anger which arise in
the body are made whole and live in joy.

24 They find their joy, their rest, and their light
completely within themselves. United with
the Lord, they attain nirvana in Brahman.

25 Healed of their sins and conflicts, working
for the good of all beings, the holy sages

26 attain nirvana in Brahman. Free from anger
and selfish desire, unified in mind, those who
follow the path of yoga and realize the Self are
established forever in that supreme state.

27 Closing their eyes, steadying their breathing,
and focusing their attention on the center of

28 spiritual consciousness, the wise master their
senses, mind, and intellect through meditation. Self-realization is their only goal. Freed
from selfish desire, fear, and anger, they live

29 in freedom always. Knowing me as the friend
of all creatures, the Lord of the universe, the
end of all offerings and all spiritual disciplines,
they attain eternal peace.

Chapter Six
The Practice of Meditation

THIS IS SURELY one of the most intriguing chapters of the Gita, for here we are given a detailed explanation of meditation addressed to the layperson. The same meditation techniques are given in more esoteric writings, such as the Yoga Sutras of Patanjali, but the Gita does it more simply, without any unnecessary mystery or complexity.

This chapter also explores the question, "Who is the true yogi?" This word *yogi,* if it has any associations for the Western reader, is likely to bring up images of rather far-out types who do strange contortions with their bodies. Yogis are still thought of as standing on their heads or reclining on a bed of nails. It is true that there are many practitioners of a kind of yoga that involves physical exercises and postures; and there are those who have achieved remarkable feats like lying on beds of nails, or even being buried alive and surviving. But this physical side of yoga (called *hatha yoga,* "the yoga of force") is not what is meant in the Gita. In fact, though physical techniques have a place, the Gita regards undue emphasis on them as extreme, not belonging to what might be called the mainstream of spiritual development.

In the Gita, the word *yogi* often has a more modest definition: it can mean a person who does his or her job with detachment from the rewards (6:1), or it can be

rendered as "one who has attained the goal of meditation." For *yogi* literally means "one who is accom-
plished in yoga," and *yoga* means "integration of the
spirit." In this sense, *yoga* means wholeness or the process of becoming whole at the deepest spiritual level.
The word *yoga* is also often used as a synonym for *raja
yoga*, the practice of meditation as taught by Patanjali;
for meditation is the direct means of becoming integrated, united with one's truest, deepest Self. Thus a
yogi, among other things, is a person who is an adept at
meditation.

Until now, Krishna has been instructing Arjuna in
the need for karma yoga, the active life of service. Now
he is ready to initiate his disciple into the practice of the
more interior disciplines of the spiritual life. Karma
yoga, he says, is the path for those who wish to climb
the mountain of Self-realization; for those who have
reached the summit, the path is *shama,* the peace of
contemplation. At the beginning of the spiritual life,
great exertion is required; as the summit is approached,
though the climb gets no easier, the dimension of contemplation or stillness is added. Many spiritual traditions, of course, use this image when speaking of the
religious quest. The mountaintop is the place where the
holy, like Moses, commune with God; and St. John of
the Cross describes the path to union with God as
climbing the mountain of Carmel.

In climbing this mountain, willpower, self-help, intense personal effort, are absolute essentials. The literal
translation of verse 5 is "one should lift oneself up by
one's Self"—a play on the word *atman,* which can mean
the highest Self as well as self in the ordinary sense.
One's self is thus one's friend or one's own enemy. The
"lower self," as Western mystics sometimes call it, is
self-will—will in the negative, selfish sense. An unruly
will twisted toward self-aggrandizement is an enemy
lurking right inside the fort, where it can do the most

THE PRACTICE OF MEDITATION

damage. But those who "have conquered themselves by themselves" have their truest friend in the Self. Only those who have genuine self-discipline, who are "self-conquered," live in peace.

These, Krishna says, are true yogis. They cannot harbor any malice, cannot even bring themselves to look upon anyone as an enemy. They are *samabuddhi*, "of equable mind." The true yogi, the person who is truly integrated inside, looks upon and feels everyone else's joy and sorrow just as if it were his own. He sees the Self in all beings, everywhere.

How is this self-conquest to be made? Very simply, the Gita teaches that the mind must be made one-pointed through the practice of meditation. This is the basic technique. In the Gita we do not see the tendency for elaboration, for ritual and mystery, that we sometimes find in the Hindu tradition. Krishna simply tells Arjuna, first, that he must find an appropriate place to meditate. A suitable spot for his practice will be clean and comfortable. In a nod to tradition, one verse recommends the meditation seat be covered with kusha grass and a deer skin—the traditional seat of the yogi. The important thing, however, is not how the meditation cushion is constructed, but what is going on in the mind. Meditation is an internal discipline to make the mind one-pointed, absolutely concentrated.

Second, Krishna offers a bit of advice about holding the body, head, and neck in a straight line. This may seem esoteric—a reference to the contortion-school of yoga—but actually it has a practical purpose. Sitting absolutely straight, with the spinal column erect, prevents drowsiness. Also, in advanced stages of meditation, it allows for the free flow of vital energy or *kundalini* (see Glossary).

Then practical advice is given: moderation is the path. Neither extreme asceticism nor indulgence will aid meditation. A superficial acquaintance with Hindu culture may leave the impression that it fosters either the sensuality of the Kama Sutra or the asceticism of the hermit. It is true that in Indian civilization we can easily see the ultimate development of the sensual and beautiful life in its finest manifestation, in painting, sculpture, music, and dance. And Indian cuisine is famous for its incredible variety of flavors and spices. India also presents us with the austere simplicity of the wandering holy man or *sadhu*. The Gita, however, recommends the middle path. Success in meditation, Krishna says, comes neither to those who eat or sleep too much nor to those who eat or sleep too little. The body should be neither overindulged nor treated harshly—the same recommendation the Buddha was to offer later, after many years of severe asceticism.

This chapter contains the famous verse (6:19) comparing the mind to a steady flame. By its very nature the untrained mind is restless, constantly wandering here and there in trying to fulfil its desires. It flickers wildly like a flame in a storm—never blown completely out, yet at the mercy of the wind. Wherever it wanders, Krishna says, it must be brought back to its source; it must learn to rest in the Self. Once it is at home in the depths of contemplation, the mind becomes steady, like an upright, unflickering flame in a windless place. In this deep meditation, and only there, can the human being find true fulfillment. Then "the still mind touches Brahman and enjoys bliss."

Now Arjuna asks the inevitable question. Krishna is way ahead of him, and the struggling disciple calls out, "Wait a minute!" or words to that effect. He says, "My mind is so restless and unsteady that I cannot even comprehend anything about this state of mystic peace you are talking about." The mind is so powerful, so turbulent, that trying to bring it under control is like trying to catch the wind.

Krishna admits that the mind is terribly hard to

train, but he maintains that it can be done through regular practice if one has detachment. It is interesting that he does not offer to help Arjuna here; that will come later. For now, he tells Arjuna that he must do it for himself, through hard work and detachment from private, personal motives.

Then Arjuna asks a rather surprising question: what happens to the person who believes in a spiritual goal but does not pursue it to the end? What if one of his more powerful compulsive desires gets the better of him, scattering his resolution the way a cloud is scattered by the wind? Arjuna must be at least partly convinced that there is something to all this, but either he is not ready to begin meditating or he is afraid that somehow he might fail if he tried. If he were to fail, he asks, would he have lost everything—all that he had given up in worldly life as well as his goal of self-fulfillment?

Affectionately, Krishna assures Arjuna that no attempt to improve his spiritual condition could possibly be a wasted effort. Even looking ahead to the next life, he has nothing to lose and everything to gain. He will be reborn in a household suitable for taking up his quest where he left off. In his next life, he will feel drawn to the spiritual goal once again, and he will have a head start. The general Hindu belief is that Self-realization requires many, many lives of spiritual discipline.

6 : The Practice of Meditation

SRI KRISHNA:

1   It is not those who lack energy or refrain
from action, but those who work without
expectation of reward who attain the goal
of meditation. Theirs is true renunciation.

2   Therefore, Arjuna, you should understand
that renunciation and the performance of
selfless service are the same. Those who
cannot renounce attachment to the results
of their work are far from the path.

3   For aspirants who want to climb the mountain of spiritual awareness, the path is selfless
work; for those who have ascended to yoga

4   the path is stillness and peace. When a person
has freed himself from attachment to the
results of work, and from desires for the
enjoyment of sense objects, he ascends to
the unitive state.

5   Reshape yourself through the power of your
will; never let yourself be degraded by self-
will. The will is the only friend of the Self,
and the will is the only enemy of the Self.

6   To those who have conquered themselves, the

will is a friend. But it is the enemy of those who have not found the Self within them.

7   The supreme Reality stands revealed in the consciousness of those who have conquered themselves. They live in peace, alike in cold and heat, pleasure and pain, praise and blame.

8   They are completely fulfilled by spiritual wisdom and Self-realization. Having conquered their senses, they have climbed to the summit of human consciousness. To such people a clod of dirt, a stone, and gold are the same.

9   They are equally disposed to family, enemies, and friends, to those who support them and those who are hostile, to the good and the evil alike. Because they are impartial, they rise to great heights.

10 Those who aspire to the state of yoga should seek the Self in inner solitude through meditation. With body and mind controlled they should constantly practice one-pointedness, free from expectations and attachment to material possessions.

11 Select a clean spot, neither too high nor too low, and seat yourself firmly on a cloth, a
12 deerskin, and kusha grass. Then, once seated, strive to still your thoughts. Make your mind one-pointed in meditation, and your heart
13 will be purified. Hold your body, head, and neck firmly in a straight line, and keep your
14 eyes from wandering. With all fears dissolved

in the peace of the Self and all desires dedicated to Brahman, controlling the mind and
fixing it on me, sit in meditation with me as
15 your only goal. With senses and mind constantly controlled through meditation, united
with the Self within, an aspirant attains nirvana, the state of abiding joy and peace in me.

16 Arjuna, those who eat too much or eat too
little, who sleep too much or sleep too little,
17 will not succeed in meditation. But those
who are temperate in eating and sleeping,
work and recreation, will come to the end of
18 sorrow through meditation. Through constant effort they learn to withdraw the mind
from selfish cravings and absorb it in the Self.
Thus they attain the state of union.

19 When meditation is mastered, the mind is
unwavering like the flame of a lamp in a
20 windless place. In the still mind, in the depths
of meditation, the Self reveals itself. Behold-
ing the Self by means of the Self, an aspirant
knows the joy and peace of complete fulfill-
21 ment. Having attained that abiding joy
beyond the senses, revealed in the stilled
mind, he never swerves from the eternal
22 truth. He desires nothing else, and cannot be
shaken by the heaviest burden of sorrow.

23 The practice of meditation frees one from all
affliction. This is the path of yoga. Follow
it with determination and sustained enthu-
24 siasm. Renouncing wholeheartedly all selfish

desires and expectations, use your will to
25 control the senses. Little by little, through
patience and repeated effort, the mind will
become stilled in the Self.

26 Wherever the mind wanders, restless and
diffuse in its search for satisfaction without,
27 lead it within; train it to rest in the Self. Abiding joy comes to those who still the mind.
Freeing themselves from the taint of self-will,
with their consciousness unified, they become
one with Brahman.

28 The infinite joy of touching Brahman is easily
attained by those who are free from the burden
of evil and established within themselves.
29 They see the Self in every creature and all creation in the Self. With consciousness unified
through meditation, they see everything
with an equal eye.

30 I am ever present to those who have realized
me in every creature. Seeing all life as my
manifestation, they are never separated from
31 me. They worship me in the hearts of all, and
all their actions proceed from me. Wherever
they may live, they abide in me.

32 When a person responds to the joys and sorrows of others as if they were his own, he has
attained the highest state of spiritual union.

ARJUNA:

33 O Krishna, the stillness of divine union which

you describe is beyond my comprehension. How can the mind, which is so restless,

34 attain lasting peace? Krishna, the mind is restless, turbulent, powerful, violent; trying to control it is like trying to tame the wind.

SRI KRISHNA:

35 It is true that the mind is restless and difficult to control. But it can be conquered, Arjuna, through regular practice and detachment.

36 Those who lack self-control will find it difficult to progress in meditation; but those who are self-controlled, striving earnestly through the right means, will attain the goal.

ARJUNA:

37 Krishna, what happens to the man who has faith but who lacks self-control and wanders from the path, not attaining success in yoga?

38 If a man becomes deluded on the spiritual path, will he lose the support of both worlds,

39 like a cloud scattered in the sky? Krishna, you can dispel all doubts; remove this doubt which binds me.

SRI KRISHNA:

40 Arjuna, my son, such a person will not be destroyed. No one who does good work will ever come to a bad end, either here or in the world to come.

41 When such people die, they go to other realms where the righteous live. They dwell there for countless years and then are reborn into a

42 home which is pure and prosperous. Or they may be born into a family where meditation is practiced; to be born into such a family is

43 extremely rare. The wisdom they have acquired in previous lives will be reawakened, Arjuna, and they will strive even harder for

44 Self-realization. Indeed, they will be driven on by the strength of their past disciplines. Even one who inquires after the practice of meditation rises above those who simply perform rituals.

45 Through constant effort over many lifetimes, a person becomes purified of all selfish desires and attains the supreme goal of life.

46 Meditation is superior to severe asceticism and the path of knowledge. It is also superior to selfless service. May you attain the goal of

47 meditation, Arjuna! Even among those who meditate, that man or woman who worships me with perfect faith, completely absorbed in me, is the most firmly established in yoga.

Chapter Seven
Wisdom from Realization

IN SANSKRIT this chapter is called literally "The Yoga of Wisdom and Realization"—or, more meaningfully, "The Yoga of Wisdom from Realization." The term used for wisdom is *jnana*; for realization, *vijnana*. There is room for confusion in this terminology, as *jnana* and *vijnana* are open to differing interpretations. Both words are from the root *jna*, "to know," which is related to the word *gnosis*. The prefix *vi* added to a noun usually intensifies its meaning; so *vijnana* could mean to know intensely or to a greater degree. In this context, however, *jnana* is the standard term for the highest kind of knowledge: not scholarship or book-learning but direct knowledge of God, spiritual wisdom. If we take *jnana* in this sense, we are not left with an obvious meaning for *vijnana*, a "more intense kind of *jnana*." Ramakrishna takes *vijnana* to mean an intimate, practical familiarity with God, the ability to carry through in daily affairs with the more abstract understanding that is *jnana*. Ramakrishna says, "He who has merely heard of fire has *ajnana*, ignorance. He who has seen fire has *jnana*. But he who has actually built a fire and cooked on it has *vijnana*."

In this chapter we find ourselves following several trails and sometimes seem to lose the unifying theme, which is knowledge of the supreme reality underlying nature. Krishna does, however, eventually come back to his starting point: knowledge contrasted with

ignorance, transcendent reality as opposed to the phenomenal world.

But to pursue the byways. First, Krishna's "two natures" are discussed. On the one hand, he has created
out of himself the elements and all things that make up
the phenomenal world. Beyond this, however, is
Krishna's spiritual nature as the transcendent Lord of
the universe. Here the Gita is referring to a concept
that later became a basis of the Sankhya school of Hindu philosophy. Sankhya recognized two fundamental
principles underlying all things: prakriti, the principle
of mind and matter, and Purusha, the principle of pure
spirit. The union of these two eternal, fundamental
forces is taken to account for the creation of the world
as we know it. Their union also shapes and defines all
ordinary human experience. In Sankhya, the goal of
Self-realization is seen as the final freeing of the spirit
(Purusha) from its flirtation with mind and matter
(prakriti). The Gita is not a technical work of philosophy, but it does put forward this basic worldview of
prakriti and Purusha.

Unlike Sankhya, however, in the Gita it is Krishna
who is behind both prakriti and Purusha. In this chapter, Krishna is presented as the Creator of the world.
His divine nature can be glimpsed here and there in his
bewildering and wonderful creation. In much Hindu
mythology, it is the god Brahma who takes credit for
creating the world. It is he, the four-faced deity, who
has flung forth the manifold worlds of this and former
(as well as future) universes. But in the mythology of
Vishnu, Brahma is born in the lotus that grows from
Vishnu's navel. The lotus is Vishnu's womb. In it
Brahma is born, and at Vishnu's urging he creates the
worlds. Vishnu is the real Creator; Brahma is a
demigod born of Vishnu's will to create. Here in the
Gita Krishna directly assumes all the roles and honors
usually shared with the other aspects of God

worshipped in the Hindu faith. It is not that these other divine personifications are rejected, but simply that all attention is on Krishna. For the author of the Gita, Krishna is the form of God to be worshipped, and for the time being all other forms of God disappear. Krishna alone is. In fact, one verse states that whatever other god one seems to worship, one is in reality approaching Krishna himself. Worshipping him, knowing him, enables the devotee to attain the goal.

Though the word is not used in the Gita, the idea of the world as Krishna's *lila,* his play, became a cherished idea of later Hinduism. Krishna, it is said, created the world in play: just as a child might desire to have companions to play with, Krishna desired companions and made the world. Krishna participates in the game of life; his divine qualities shine through in the world wherever there is excellence of any kind. He is, he tells Arjuna, the essence of every created thing: the sapidity of water, the brightness of fire, the effort of the spiritual aspirant. This happy view of the world may be what is meant by the *vijnana* of our title—the mystic's vision of the divine as present here and now is perhaps the real meaning of the term.

The word *maya* appears here, though not for the first time in the Gita. Just as the concepts of prakriti and Purusha are later developed in Sankhya philosophy, *maya* is later built into the formal structure of Vedanta, another of the six major schools of Indian philosophy. The word *maya* comes from the root *ma,* "to measure out," and originally meant the power of a deity to create, especially to create what Indian philosophy calls "name and form": matter and its percepts. Maya was the magical capacity to create form and illusion—a god's divine power to put on a disguise, or to fling forth world after world of life. Maya is also the outward look of things, the passing show that conceals immortal being. Maya can be both delightful and dangerous, alluring and yet death-dealing. The gunas, the three basic qualities of all created things, swirl within the world of maya. Crossing beyond maya, the "passing show" of phenomena, is the goal of the wise voyager, and one bridge is devotion. In this chapter the Gita begins to stress the importance of love and devotion—themes that later become dominant.

Krishna's true nature is hidden by maya (7: 25). The dangers of maya are not depicted strongly in this chapter, but the "delusions"—*moha*—of life in maya's world are hinted at; they are, essentially, the self-centered attachments Krishna has been warning against. *Moha*, which means confusion or delusion, is something like dreaming while awake, "living in a dream." The duality of attachment and aversion (love and hate) beguiles the mind into this *moha*-swoon right at birth, "from the very start" (7:27). Knowing Krishna, and devotion to him, is the way beyond this delusion. Thus Chapter 7 contrasts wisdom (*jnana* and *vijnana*) with the delusion (*moha*) of spiritual ignorance.

We find here many seminal ideas that are elaborated in the later philosophies of Sankhya and Vedanta. These concepts of prakriti, Purusha, and maya do not originate with the Gita, however. The word *maya* appears in the Rig Veda, the most ancient of the Vedas, and Purusha is a recurring theme in the Upanishads. The Gita is a halfway point between the spontaneous insights of the Upanishads and the later, highly formalized philosophical systems. In the Gita we find a fairly organized presentation of these and other key concepts without a cumbersome technical explanation.

7 : *Wisdom from Realization*

1 With your mind intent on me, Arjuna, discipline yourself with the practice of yoga. Depend on me completely. Listen, and I will dispel all your doubts; you will come to know me fully and be united with me.

2 I will give you both jnana and vijnana. When both these are realized, there is nothing more you need to know.

3 One person in many thousands may seek perfection, yet of these only a few reach the
4 goal and come to realize me. Earth, water, fire, air, *akasha,* mind, intellect, and ego— these are the eight divisions of my prakriti.
5 But beyond this I have another, higher nature, Arjuna; it supports the whole universe and is the source of life in all beings.

6 In these two aspects of my nature is the womb of all creation. The birth and dissolution of the cosmos itself take place in me.
7 There is nothing that exists separate from me, Arjuna. The entire universe is suspended from me as my necklace of jewels.

8   Arjuna, I am the taste of pure water and the
     radiance of the sun and moon. I am the sacred
     word and the sound heard in air, and the cour-
9   age of human beings. I am the sweet fragrance
     in the earth and the radiance of fire; I am the
     life in every creature and the striving of the
     spiritual aspirant.

10   My eternal seed, Arjuna, is to be found in
     every creature. I am the power of discrimina-
     tion in those who are intelligent, and the glory
11   of the noble. In those who are strong, I am
     strength, free from passion and selfish attach-
     ment. I am desire itself, if that desire is in
     harmony with the purpose of life.

12   The states of sattva, rajas, and tamas come
13   from me, but I am not in them. These three
     gunas deceive the world: people fail to look
     beyond them to me, supreme and imperish-
14   able. The three gunas make up my divine
     maya, difficult to overcome. But they cross
15   over this maya who take refuge in me. Others
     are deluded by maya; performing evil deeds,
     they have no devotion to me. Having lost all
     discrimination, they follow the way of their
     lower nature.

16   Good people come to worship me for differ-
     ent reasons. Some come to the spiritual life
     because of suffering, some in order to under-
     stand life; some come through a desire to
     achieve life's purpose, and some come who

17 are men and women of wisdom. Unwavering
    in devotion, always united with me, the man
    or woman of wisdom surpasses all the others.
    To them I am the dearest beloved, and they
18 are very dear to me. All those who follow the
    spiritual path are blessed. But the wise who
    are always established in union, for whom
    there is no higher goal than me, may be re-
    garded as my very Self.

19 After many births the wise seek refuge in
    me, seeing me everywhere and in every-
20 thing. Such great souls are very rare. There
    are others whose discrimination is misled by
    many desires. Following their own nature,
    they worship lower gods, practicing various
    rites.

21 When a person is devoted to something with
22 complete faith, I unify his faith in that. Then,
    when his faith is completely unified, he gains
    the object of his devotion. In this way, every
23 desire is fulfilled by me. Those whose under-
    standing is small attain only transient satisfac-
    tion: those who worship the gods go to the
    gods. But my devotees come to me.

24 Through lack of understanding, people
    believe that I, the Unmanifest, have entered
    into some form. They fail to realize my true
25 nature, which transcends birth and death. Few
    see through the veil of maya. The world, de-
    luded, does not know that I am without birth

26 and changeless. I know everything about the
past, the present, and the future, Arjuna; but
there is no one who knows me completely.

27 Delusion arises from the duality of attraction and aversion, Arjuna; every creature is
28 deluded by these from birth. But those who
have freed themselves from all wrongdoing
are firmly established in worship of me. Their
actions are pure, and they are free from the
delusion caused by the pairs of opposites.

29 Those who take refuge in me, striving for
liberation from old age and death, come to
know Brahman, the Self, and the nature of all
30 action. Those who see me ruling the cosmos,
who see me in the *adhibhuta*, the *adhidaiva*, and
the *adhiyajna*, are conscious of me even at the
time of death.

Chapter Eight
The Eternal Godhead

THIS CHAPTER alludes briefly to several important concepts presented more fully in the Upanishads. The presentation in this chapter is so sketchy that it will be helpful to quote the Upanishads to elucidate these points. Also, this chapter is rather curious in that it presents a very ancient view of the soul's journey after death. These ideas about the afterlife did not originate in the Gita, and probably are even more ancient than the Upanishads. Another ancient concept here is that of a cyclical universe, which is elaborated in other Hindu scriptures in great detail; this chapter merely refers to it in passing.

The chapter begins with Arjuna asking what appear to be questions of theology, but the role of theologian does not fit him very naturally. These questions are asked in response to the technical terms mentioned in the last verse of Chapter 7. The sense of Krishna's answer is in accord with what he said earlier about his maya: he is God immanent in all things as well as God transcendent.

But it is Arjuna's other question that determines the direction the discourse now takes. Arjuna asks how Krishna can be known at the hour of death. Here, of course, Arjuna means Krishna in his cosmic, mystical aspect, so he is asking in effect, "How can the Self-realized person enter the supreme state of immortality at the time of death?" Krishna replies that whoever remembers him at the time of death will enter *mad-bhavam,* "my being." If Arjuna can remember Krishna in the hour of death, he will be united with Krishna and enter into immortality.

In fact, whatever it may be, the content of the mind at the hour of death directs the soul in its journey to rebirth. Thus the mind influences the evolution of the soul as it moves into the next life. Whatever a person thinks about in life—his or her deepest motivations—are likely to be the last thoughts at the time of death. So there is a continuity between this life and the next, and all the baggage of desire and motivation goes right along with the soul. But here Krishna is talking about the person—he hopes it will be Arjuna—who has no worldly baggage, who will remember Krishna at the final hour.

To make sure he focuses his devotion on Krishna at the hour of death, Arjuna should make a practice of remembering him continually now. If he makes his mind one-pointed in meditation and learns to focus his being on Krishna, then naturally at the time of death he will think of nothing else. Otherwise, in the chaos of death, he will panic and lose his way.

Krishna describes in detail what happens to consciousness at the moment of death (8:12–13). These verses actually describe the yogi as being in control of the process of death. Directing his consciousness step by step through the difficult ordeal of leaving the body, he attains the supreme goal. This idea is also accepted by one of the greatest teachers of meditation in ancient India, Patanjali, who says in the Yoga Sutras that the yogi dies at will. Similar descriptions of the death process occur in the Upanishads, though there the dying person is not necessarily in control. Since the Upanishads are more detailed, they are worth quoting here:

When the Self seems to become weak and sink into

unconsciousness, the vital breaths gather to him. Then he takes with him those particles of light and descends into the heart. When the consciousness that is in the eye turns back, the dying man no longer sees any form. "He is becoming one," they say; "he does not see." "He is becoming one," they say; "he does not smell." "He is becoming one," they say; "he does not taste." "He is becoming one," they say; "he does not speak." "He is becoming one," they say; "he does not hear." "He is becoming one," they say; "he does not think or touch or know." The point of his heart lights up, and by that light the Self departs, either through the eye, or the skull, or through some other door of the body. And when he departs, life departs: and when life departs, all other vital forces depart after it. He is conscious, and with consciousness he leaves the body. Then his knowledge and his works and his previous impressions go along with him. (Brihad. Up. 4:4:1-2)

First consciousness is withdrawn from the senses. The dying person no longer hears or sees what is going on around him. He is still conscious, but the "light" of consciousness has been withdrawn from the senses, here called the "gates" of the body. There are said to be nine such gates: two eyes, two nostrils, two ears, the mouth, and the organs of generation and excretion. Sometimes two more are added: the navel and the sagittal suture, located at the top of the skull and called in Sanskrit *brahmarandhra,* "the aperture of Brahman."

When consciousness has been withdrawn from these gates, Krishna says, "the mind is placed ['locked up'] in the heart." (8:12) Here, as in Christian mysticism, it is the heart and not the head that is taken to be the home of the soul. Probably what is meant is the heart *chakra,* the center of consciousness corresponding to the center of the chest. *Prana* (vital energy) and aware-ness have been withdrawn from the outer frontiers of personality and consolidated within. At this stage of the death process an ordinary person has no access to the will; but it is just here that *prana*, with conscious awareness, must be made to move upwards to the head. If *prana* leaves the body through the *brahmaran-dhra*, there will be no rebirth: that is, the dying person will enter samadhi at the time of death. In samadhi, prana is withdrawn from lower levels of awareness to rush upwards to the seventh center at the crown of the head. This is possible only for the yogi who has thoroughly mastered meditation and the control of prana. If prana exits through some other one of the eleven doors of the body, the Upanishads say, the state of immortality will not be gained:

> When he departs from this body, he ascends with the rays of the sun, repeating the syllable *Om*. As soon as he thinks of it, he comes to the sun. That, indeed, is the door to the next world. Those who know enter; those who do not know are stopped. There is a verse:

> A hundred and one subtle tracts lead from the heart;
> One of these goes upwards to the crown of the head.
> Going up by it, he goes to eternal life.
> Others depart in various directions.
>   (Chan. Up. 8:6:5–6)

In the Gita, as well as in this passage from the Chandogya Upanishad, the mantram *Om* is mentioned. If the yogi can remember the mantram even as consciousness itself is departing the body—and, the Gita adds, if he can meditate on Krishna—he will go to the "highest goal." Relinquishing the body in a state of samadhi, he attains the mystic eternity that is union with Krishna.

In this chapter the Gita briefly touches upon the two paths, "northern" and "southern," that the soul may take after death. Verses 24–25 present in abbreviated form what the Brihadaranyaka Upanishad spells out in obscure detail:

Those who know this, who meditate upon Truth with faith while living in the forest , go to the light, from light to day, from day to the fortnight of the moon's waxing, from the waxing fortnight to the six months of the sun's northern journey, from those six months to the world of the devas, from the world of the devas to the sun, from the sun to the lightning. Then a spirit approaches them and leads them to the world of Brahman. In that world they live for eternal ages. They do not return again.

But those who conquer worlds through sacrifice, charity, and austerity pass into the smoke, from the smoke into the night, from the night into the fortnight of the waning moon, from the fortnight of the waning moon into the six months of the sun's southern journey, from there into the world of the ancestors, from the world of the ancestors into the moon, . . . and from there to rebirth. (Brihad. Up. 6:2:15–16)

"Northern and southern paths" refers to the path of the sun, which moves northward after the winter solstice and southward after the summer solstice. To die during the period in which the sun is moving southward was considered inauspicious; dying during the period after the winter solstice, when the sun is moving back north, meant the soul might take the northern path which leads to immortality. In the Gita and the Upanishads, this "northern path" has come to signify that the soul has been released from karma and need not be reborn. The southern path, by contrast, leads the soul to a new birth in this world, a birth suitable to its karma. This view of the soul's journey after death has a primordial quality about it, giving the feeling that it far predates even the Upanishads. Perhaps it is a belief of very ancient times that found its way into the Upanishads, which say that the spiritually ready soul makes the journey of the northern route while those who have only practiced rituals take the southern.

This chapter also briefly alludes to the Days and Nights of Brahma. Brahma is the Creator of the Hindu trinity, who brings forth the cosmos at the will of Vishnu. But Brahma in a sense is not in control of this creative process. Just as day follows night in eternal, unvarying rhythm, so does the entire universe undergo cycles of creation, death, and new birth. As the Day of Brahma dawns, the cosmos comes into being; as the Day comes to an end, the entire creation dies and ceases to exist. Then, for a Night as long as the cosmic Day, the universe rests. It ceases to be—or, rather, it continues only in a subtle, unmanifest form, a dream in the mind of Vishnu, who lies sleeping on the waves of the cosmic night. Then, without deviating from the cosmic rhythm, the cosmos is reborn when the Night is over. The new universe dawns, and Brahma once again moves into his active, creative Day.

Scholars have noted that this grand vision of the cosmos being born, dying, and being reborn for eternity—cosmos after cosmos arising from the black immensity of nothingness—is quite similar to modern theories of the expanding and contracting universe put forward by contemporary cosmology. The vast time spans accepted by present-day physics are also similar to the cosmic Days and Nights of Brahma. Each Day lasts for a thousand yugas, which equals 4,320,000,000 years. For this near-eternity of time the universe lives and grows; then it dies and lies dormant for an equal time, before the new Day dawns.

There is a state of being, however, that is higher than the perishable cosmos, which is not born and does not die the cosmic death. Here (8:20) it is called simply *avyakta*, the Unmanifest. This is the supreme goal of all living things, and it is Krishna's home (8:21). Returning to this final resting place, the soul enters into immortal bliss and is not reborn.

8 : The Eternal Godhead

ARJUNA:

1 O Krishna, what is Brahman, and what is the
nature of action? What is the *adhyatma*, the
adhibhuta, the *adhidaiva*?

2 What is the *adhiyajna*, the supreme sacrifice,
and how is it to be offered? How are the self-
controlled united with you at the time of
death?

SRI KRISHNA:

3 My highest nature, the imperishable Brahman, gives every creature its existence and
lives in every creature as the adhyatma. My
action is creation and the bringing forth of
4 creatures. The adhibhuta is the perishable
body; the adhidaiva is Purusha, eternal spirit.
The adhiyajna, the supreme sacrifice, is made
to me as the Lord within you.

5 Those who remember me at the time of death
6 will come to me. Do not doubt this. Whatever
occupies the mind at the time of death determines the destination of the dying; always
they will tend toward that state of being.
7 Therefore, remember me at all times and fight

on. With your heart and mind intent on me,
8   you will surely come to me. When you make
your mind one-pointed through regular practice of meditation, you will find the supreme
glory of the Lord.

9   The Lord is the supreme poet, the first cause,
the sovereign ruler, subtler than the tiniest
particle, the support of all, inconceivable,
10   bright as the sun, beyond darkness. Remembering him in this way at the time of death,
through devotion and the power of meditation, with your mind completely stilled and
your concentration fixed in the center of
spiritual awareness between the eyebrows,
you will realize the supreme Lord.

11   I will tell you briefly of the eternal state all
scriptures affirm, which can be entered only
by those who are self-controlled and free from
selfish passions. Those whose lives are dedicated to Brahman attain this supreme goal.

12   Remembering me at the time of death, close
down the doors of the senses and place the
mind in the heart. Then, while absorbed in
meditation, focus all energy upwards to the
13   head. Repeating in this state the divine Name,
the syllable *Om* that represents the changeless
Brahman, you will go forth from the body
and attain the supreme goal.

14   I am easily attained by the person who always
remembers me and is attached to nothing else.

15 Such a person is a true yogi, Arjuna. Great
    souls make their lives perfect and discover me;
    they are freed from mortality and the suffer-
16 ing of this separate existence. Every creature
    in the universe is subject to rebirth, Arjuna,
    except the one who is united with me.

17 Those who understand the cosmic laws know
    that the Day of Brahma ends after a thousand
    yugas and the Night of Brahma ends after a
18 thousand yugas. When the day of Brahma
    dawns, forms are brought forth from the Un-
    manifest; when the night of Brahma comes,
19 these forms merge in the Formless again. This
    multitude of beings is created and destroyed
    again and again in the succeeding days and
20 nights of Brahma. But beyond this formless
    state there is another, unmanifested reality,
    which is eternal and is not dissolved when the
21 cosmos is destroyed. Those who realize life's
    supreme goal know that I am unmanifested
    and unchanging. Having come home to me,
    they never return to separate existence.

22 This supreme Lord who pervades all exis-
    tence, the true Self of all creatures, may be
    realized through undivided love.

23 There are two paths, Arjuna, which the soul
    may follow at the time of death. One leads to
    rebirth and the other to liberation.

24 The six months of the northern path of the
    sun, the path of light, of fire, of day, of the

bright fortnight, leads knowers of Brahman
25 to the supreme goal. The six months of the
southern path of the sun, the path of smoke,
of night, of the dark fortnight, leads other
souls to the light of the moon and to rebirth.

26 These two paths, the light and the dark, are
said to be eternal, leading some to liberation
27 and others to rebirth. Once you have known
these two paths, Arjuna, you can never be deluded again. Attain this knowledge through
28 perseverance in yoga. There is merit in study-
ing the scriptures, in selfless service, austerity,
and giving, but the practice of meditation
carries you beyond all these to the supreme
abode of the highest Lord.

Chapter Nine
The Royal Path

THIS CHAPTER praises Krishna as the Supreme Being who has created the world and dwells immanent in his creation. Krishna's exalted nature is stressed, and warning is given to the person who thinks that God is limited to his creation. It is true that Krishna has taken on a human form, but those who see only a limited human being and show him disrespect are courting great spiritual harm. These verses contain a warning for those who would underestimate Krishna's divine power.

In this chapter Krishna replaces the many gods and goddesses of the usual Hindu pantheon, each of which represents a different divine power; here Krishna is seen as containing within himself all such powers. It is Krishna and Krishna alone who is to be worshipped: he is the goal, the support, the only refuge, the one true friend; he is the beginning and the end (9:18).

It follows that those who practice a ritual religion, offering the ritual sacrifices ordained by the Vedas, do not attain the true goal of their lives. True, they do enjoy heaven after death. But when their store of merit is used up, they are born again on this earth in order to have another chance at turning away from personal gain and aiming at life's supreme goal. So long as they are motivated only by self-centered desires they must be born again and again, and their spiritual evolution either stands still or they make very little progress.

Even these souls, however, are really worshipping Krishna, though they do not know it. They seek Krishna, the Supreme Being, in all their wanderings through many, many lives and even in their sojourns in heaven, where they enjoy the reward of their good deeds. Because they do not know his real nature, however, they will not attain the goal, but will be reborn.

An endless round of rebirths may seem like a living damnation of the struggling soul—a harsh note that would be uncharacteristic of the Gita. But this is not a question of damnation. The purpose of life is to realize God, and until this is done, the soul cannot escape creating more karma which has to be worked out, however many lives it might take. The choice to turn toward Self-realization is always open.

The Gita does not dwell on this, however, but quickly goes on to reveal Krishna's more compassionate nature. It makes the point that whatever a person deeply desires—whatever he or she worships—will eventually be attained, in some life or other. In particular, to have real, selfless love, regardless of the object, *is* to love Krishna, the ultimate good. This kind of love, called *bhakti* in Sanskrit, is far more potent than all the observances of conventional religiosity—a point the Gita is slowly coming round to. But to have this devotion without understanding Krishna's nature is not enough. In the end, to attain his goal, Arjuna must have devotion *and* understand it is Krishna's universal aspect that he loves. Then he will truly attain the eternal, immortal state.

This chapter contains a famous and very popular series of verses:

> Whatever you do, make it an offering to me—the food you eat, the sacrifices you make, the help you give, even your suffering. In this way you will be freed from the bondage of karma, and from its results both pleasant and painful. (9:27–28)

Krishna accepts every offering made to him in the right spirit; he assures Arjuna of this. Then he demands that Arjuna make everything—every act, every meal, every sacrifice, every gift, even his sufferings—an offering to God. He demands this so that Arjuna can be released from the bondage of karma. This is a new emphasis, a new way. If Arjuna can live in complete union with Krishna's will, doing everything for Krishna alone, then by that very purity of will he will be free from selfish motives and thus released from karma. His spirit will be free, and he will attain his goal of mystic union with Krishna.

Krishna declares that he is impartial to all creatures: he neither favors nor rejects anyone. It is their sincere love that is important. Those who are truly devoted to Krishna live in him, and he abides in them. With some daring, probably at the risk of discomfort to the more orthodox, Krishna adds that even a sinner who takes wholehearted refuge in him becomes good. The word used is *sadhu,* which literally means a good person but has come to signify one who leads the spiritual life, giving up all personal goals to achieve the final goal. The word for sinner, *sudurachara,* should not be passed by either. *Su* is literally "good"; *dur* is "bad": thus "one whose conduct is *really* bad," as we might say "good and hot" to mean *really* hot.

Krishna promises that his devotees must attain peace at last. No one who has genuine love and devotion can perish. The meaning here is taken to be "perish" in a spiritual sense, come to spiritual harm. The message of this chapter is simple. It contains no philosophy and only a little theology. The one message is: have real love, love for the Lord of Love who is in all creatures, and you will in the end attain the goal. This is the royal secret that Krishna had promised to reveal.

9 : The Royal Path

SRI KRISHNA:

1 Because of your faith, I shall tell you the most profound of secrets: obtaining both jnana and vijnana, you will be free from all evil.

2 This royal knowledge, this royal secret, is the greatest purifier. Righteous and imperishable, it is a joy to practice and can be directly experi-
3 enced. But those who have no faith in the supreme law of life do not find me, Arjuna. They return to the world, passing from death to death.

4 I pervade the entire universe in my unmanifested form. All creatures find their existence
5 in me, but I am not limited by them. Behold my divine mystery! These creatures do not really dwell in me, and though I bring them forth and support them, I am not confined
6 within them. They move in me as the winds move in every direction in space.

7 At the end of the eon these creatures return to unmanifested matter; at the beginning of the
8 next cycle I send them forth again. Controlling my prakriti, again and again I bring forth

9   these myriad forms and subject them to the laws of prakriti. None of these actions bind me, Arjuna. I am unattached to them, so they do not disturb my nature.

10   Under my watchful eye the laws of nature take their course. Thus is the world set in motion; thus the animate and the inanimate are created.

11   The foolish do not look beyond physical appearances to see my true nature as the Lord
12   of all creation. The knowledge of such deluded people is empty; their lives are fraught with disaster and evil and their work and hopes are all in vain.

13   But truly great souls seek my divine nature. They worship me with a one-pointed mind, having realized that I am the eternal source of
14   all. Constantly striving, they make firm their resolve and worship me without wavering. Full of devotion, they sing of my divine glory.

15   Others follow the path of jnana, spiritual wisdom. They see that where there is One, that One is me; where there are many, all are me; they see my face everywhere.

16   I am the ritual and the sacrifice; I am true medicine and the mantram. I am the offering and the fire which consumes it, and he to whom it is offered.

17 I am the father and mother of this universe,
and its grandfather too; I am its entire support. I am the sum of all knowledge, the
purifier, the syllable *Om*; I am the sacred
scriptures, the Rik, Yajur, and Sama Vedas.

18 I am the goal of life, the Lord and support of
all, the inner witness, the abode of all. I am
the only refuge, the one true friend; I am the
beginning, the staying, and the end of
creation; I am the womb and the eternal seed.

19 I am heat; I give and withhold the rain. I am
immortality and I am death; I am what is and
what is not.

20 Those who follow the rituals given in the
Vedas, who offer sacrifices and take soma,
free themselves from evil and attain the vast
heaven of the gods, where they enjoy celestial
21 pleasures. When they have enjoyed these fully,
their merit is exhausted and they return to this
land of death. Thus observing Vedic rituals but
caught in an endless chain of desires, they
come and go.

22 Those who worship me and meditate on me
constantly, without any other thought, I will
provide for all their needs.

23 Those who worship other gods with faith and
devotion also worship me, Arjuna, even if
24 they do not observe the usual forms. I am the
object of all worship, its enjoyer and Lord.

But those who fail to realize my true nature
25   must be reborn. Those who worship the
devas will go to the realm of the devas; those
who worship their ancestors will be united
with them after death. Those who worship
phantoms will become phantoms; but my
devotees will come to me.

26   Whatever I am offered in devotion with a
pure heart—a leaf, a flower, fruit, or water—
27   I partake of that love offering. Whatever you
do, make it an offering to me—the food you
eat, the sacrifices you make, the help you
28   give, even your suffering. In this way you will
be freed from the bondage of karma, and
from its results both pleasant and painful.
Then, firm in renunciation and yoga, with
your heart free, you will come to me.

29   I look upon all creatures equally; none are
less dear to me and none more dear. But those
who worship me with love live in me, and I
come to life in them.

30   Even a sinner becomes holy when he worships
me alone with firm resolve. Quickly his
31   soul conforms to dharma and he attains to
boundless peace. Never forget this, Arjuna:
no one who is devoted to me will ever
come to harm.

32   All those who take refuge in me, whatever
their birth, race, sex, or caste, will attain the
supreme goal; this realization can be attained

33 even by those whom society scorns. Kings and sages too seek this goal with devotion. Therefore, having been born in this transient and forlorn world, give all your love to me.

34 Fill your mind with me; love me; serve me; worship me always. Seeking me in your heart, you will at last be united with me.

Chapter Ten
Divine Splendor

KRISHNA goes deeper into the revelation of his divine being, revealing himself as the source from which all things come, the One who is the reality behind the many. Though the source of all virtues, he is also the ultimate reality that transcends all opposites. Thus he is both happiness and suffering, birth and death, being and nonbeing. Like the Brahman of the Upanishads, he is beyond duality, utterly beyond the constricting categories of the things of this world. His true nature is beyond the reach of thought. He can only be known in the state of samadhi, where knower and known become one.

Arjuna calls Krishna *Purushottama,* "the supreme Purusha," "the supreme Person." Krishna is now no human charioteer but Bhagavan, "the munificent Lord"; and Arjuna, leaving his warrior persona behind, now stands revealed as a seeker after truth. At Arjuna's request, Krishna now reveals a few of his divine powers and attributes (*vibhuti*s).

From this point on the chapter becomes difficult for non-Hindus because of the many unfamiliar names that are mentioned. The idea throughout is that in whatever category, Krishna is the chief, the best, the most intense, the most beautiful, the most awesome, the essence. Many of the allusions will be familiar—for example, among rivers Krishna is the Ganges. But many of the names come from Hindu mythology and are not so well known. There is no room here to explain every name, but the following paragraphs will pick up a few of importance.

First, Krishna is the Atman, the inner Self in all beings. It is fitting that this be mentioned first, for of all his myriad manifestations this is the most important, at least to the struggling spiritual aspirant that is Arjuna. Krishna is Arjuna's innermost Self, and that is how he is to be known in contemplation. Of all the forms in which to meditate upon Krishna, the Atman is mentioned first.

Krishna is Vishnu, the great compassionate, sustaining God of the Hindu faith. It is Vishnu who cares so much about the sufferings of Mother Earth and her children that he comes to earth again and again, in age after age, to relieve oppression and renew righteousness.

Krishna is the sun, worshipped in India since ancient times. He is Indra, the chief of the Vedic gods, who wanes in importance as Indian culture becomes more introspective. Indra is the god of storm and battle, who hurls the thunderbolt against the enemies of the gods. In Vedic religion he is a mighty lord, not to be trifled with, but later on he must admit defeat at the hands of Krishna, who protects the people from Indra's stormy wrath.

Krishna is also Shankara, the more beneficent aspect of the awesome deity Rudra, better known as Shiva. Among mountains Krishna is Meru, the high mountain home of Shiva and the other gods, the highest peak and center of the world. Krishna is consciousness, the syllable *Om*, and the mantram or Holy Name. He is the mythic horse and the fabulous elephant that were produced when the cosmic ocean was churned for the elixir of immortality.

Krishna is Ananta, the cosmic serpent on which Lord Vishnu sleeps. He is Varuna, Vedic god of the oceans, and Yama, the god of death (the name means "the controller"); among demons (*asura*s) he is Prahlada, who, though born in the race of demons, was devoted to God and never swayed in his love, even when his own father tried to kill him. And of course Krishna is Rama, the great warrior prince—also an incarnation of Vishnu—whose exploits are told in the immortal epic, the Ramayana.

Of all fields of knowledge, Krishna says, he is knowledge of the Self. But the study of Sanskrit and its grammar were important in ancient India, and Krishna doesn't neglect this field. He is *A* among letters; among compound words he is the *dvandva,* which joins equals. He is the *gayatri*—perhaps a particular meter found in the poetry of the Vedas, but generally taken to be a famous prayer from the Rig Veda (3:62:10) composed in that meter, which has been chanted every morning by countless worshippers for three thousand years.

It is fitting that among seasons Krishna is the spring, the season of flowers. Less easily understood is his claim to be the gambling of gamblers. The word for gamblers here has a hint of "fraudulent"; it might be loosely translated as "cardsharps." Krishna has a sense of play, and as gambling is the obsession of the gambler, it seems natural that Krishna might claim this as a *vibhuti.* Also, in ancient India gambling was considered a royal pastime, and no king of repute would refuse a friendly game of dice.

In the human realm, Krishna is the "son of Vasudeva," a prince of the Vrishni line—in other words, the human form that is Arjuna's friend and charioteer. He is also Arjuna! And he is Vyasa, the composer of the Gita—indeed, of the whole Mahabharata.

Wherever Arjuna finds strength, beauty, or power, Krishna concludes, he should recognize it as coming from a spark of Krishna's glory. Then, after no doubt overwhelming his friend Arjuna with this stupendous list of divine powers and revelations, he asks casually, "But what use is it to know all of these details? The important fact is to know that I am, and that a tiny portion of my being supports all things."

10 : Divine Splendor

SRI KRISHNA:

1 Listen further, Arjuna, to my supreme
teaching, which gives you such joy. Desiring
your welfare, O strong-armed warrior, I will
tell you more.

2 Neither gods nor sages know my origin, for I
am the source from which the gods and sages
3 come. Whoever knows me as the Lord of all
creation, without birth or beginning, knows
the truth and frees himself from all evil.

4 Discrimination, wisdom, understanding,
forgiveness, truth, self-control, and peace of
mind; pleasure and pain, birth and death, fear
5 and courage, honor and infamy; nonviolence,
charity, equanimity, contentment, and
perseverance in spiritual disciplines—all the
different qualities found in living creatures
have their source in me.

6 The seven great sages and the four ancient
ancestors were born from my mind and re-
7 ceived my power. From them came all the creatures of this world. Whoever understands my
power and the mystery of my manifestations
comes without doubt to be united with me.

8 I am the source from which all creatures
evolve. The wise remember this and worship
9 me with loving devotion. Their thoughts are
all absorbed in me, and all their vitality flows
to me. Teaching one another, talking about
me always, they are happy and fulfilled.

10 To those steadfast in love and devotion I give
spiritual wisdom, so that they may come to
11 me. Out of compassion I destroy the darkness
of their ignorance. From within them I light
the lamp of wisdom and dispel all darkness
from their lives.

ARJUNA:

12 You are Brahman supreme, the highest
abode, the supreme purifier, the divine,
eternal spirit, first among the gods, unborn
13 and infinite. The great sages and seers—
Narada, Asita, Devala, and Vyasa too—have
acclaimed you thus; now you have declared
it to me yourself.

14 Now, O Krishna, I believe that everything
you have told me is divine truth. O Lord,
neither gods nor demons know your real
15 nature. Indeed, you alone know yourself,
O supreme spirit. You are the source of
being and the master of every creature, God
of gods, the Lord of the universe.

16 Tell me all your divine attributes, leaving
nothing unsaid. Tell me of the glories with
17 which you fill the cosmos. Krishna, you are

a supreme master of yoga. Tell me how I
should meditate to gain constant awareness of
you. In what things and in what ways should
18 I meditate on you? O Krishna, you who stir
up people's hearts, tell me in detail your attributes and your powers; I can never tire of
hearing your immortal words.

SRI KRISHNA:

19 All right, Arjuna, I will tell you of my
divine powers. I will mention only the most
glorious; for there is no end to them.

20 I am the true Self in the heart of every
creature, Arjuna, and the beginning, middle,
and end of their existence.

21 Among the shining gods I am Vishnu; of
luminaries I am the sun; among the storm
gods I am Marichi, and in the night sky I am
the moon.

22 Among scriptures I am the Sama Veda, and
among the lesser gods I am Indra. Among the
senses I am the mind, and in living beings I
am consciousness.

23 Among the Rudras I am Shankara. Among
the spirits of the natural world I am Kubera,
god of wealth, and Pavaka, the purifying fire.
Among mountains I am Meru.

24 Among priests I am Brihaspati, and among
military leaders I am Skanda. Among bodies
of water I am the ocean.

25 Among the great seers I am Bhrigu, and
among words, the syllable *Om*; I am the
repetition of the Holy Name, and among
mountains I am the Himalayas.

26 Among trees I am the *ashvattha,* the sacred fig;
among the *gandharva*s or heavenly musicians I
am Chitraratha. Among divine seers I am
Narada, and among sages I am Kapila.

27 I was born from the nectar of immortality
as the primordial horse and as Indra's noble
elephant. Among men, I am the king.

28 Among weapons I am the thunderbolt. I am
Kamadhuk, the cow that fulfills all desires; I
am Kandarpa, the power of sex, and Vasuki,
the king of snakes.

29 I am Ananta, the cosmic serpent, and Varuna,
the god of water; I am Aryaman among the
noble ancestors. Among the forces which
restrain I am Yama, the god of death.

30 Among animals I am the lion; among birds,
the eagle Garuda. I am Prahlada, born among
the demons, and of all that measures, I am
time.

31 Among purifying forces I am the wind;
among warriors, Rama. Of water creatures
I am the crocodile, and of rivers I am the
Ganges.

32 I am the beginning, middle, and end of creation. Of all the sciences I am the science of
Self-knowledge, and I am logic in those who
33 debate. Among letters I am *A*; among gram-
matical compounds I am the dvandva. I am
infinite time, and the sustainer whose face is
seen everywhere.

34 I am death, which overcomes all, and the
source of all beings still to be born. I am the
feminine qualities: fame, beauty, perfect
speech, memory, intelligence, loyalty, and
forgiveness.

35 Among the hymns of the Sama Veda I am the
Brihat; among poetic meters, the Gayatri.
Among months I am Margashirsha, first of
the year; among seasons I am spring, that
brings forth flowers.

36 I am the gambling of the gambler and the
radiance in all that shines. I am effort, I am
victory, and I am the goodness of the
virtuous.

37 Among the Vrishnis I am Krishna, and
among the Pandavas I am Arjuna. Among
sages I am Vyasa, and among poets, Ushanas.

38 I am the scepter which metes out punishment,
and the art of statesmanship in those who
lead. I am the silence of the unknown and the
wisdom of the wise.

39 I am the seed that can be found in every
creature, Arjuna; for without me nothing
can exist, neither animate nor inanimate.

40 But there is no end to my divine attributes,
Arjuna; these I have mentioned are only a
41 few. Wherever you find strength, or beauty,
or spiritual power, you may be sure that these
have sprung from a spark of my essence.

42 But of what use is it to you to know all this,
Arjuna? Just remember that I am, and that I
support the entire cosmos with only a fragment of my being.

Chapter Eleven
The Cosmic Vision

THIS IS THE most exalted chapter of the entire Gita, for here Arjuna sees the divine vision of Krishna in his full nature as God himself, Lord of the Universe. It is difficult to see at first why the ultimate spiritual vision should be granted to Arjuna at this point. We must remember that Krishna and Arjuna have been companions for many lives. Yet at the opening of the Gita, Arjuna is a warrior, little concerned with mystic visions. Step by step Krishna has led him to an understanding of the real purpose of his life— to know who he is and to know also who Krishna is. In the last chapter, Krishna had reached the point where he was willing to reveal to Arjuna the manifestations of divine power. Arjuna had not only asked about those powers, but had even wanted to know in which forms he might meditate on Krishna—the first time Arjuna had spoken of contemplation.

Now, in Chapter 11, Arjuna asks to see Krishna as He really is. His desire is granted, and in essence the rest of the chapter describes Arjuna's samadhi. *Samadhi* is the word used by Patanjali in his classic work, the Yoga Sutras, to describe the final stage in meditation, in which the mind is completely concentrated and a superconscious mode of knowing comes into play. Patanjali speaks of many different kinds of samadhi, but for practical purposes we may speak of two kinds only: *savikalpa* and *nirvikalpa*. Arjuna's vision begins with savikalpa samadhi, in which he sees God in a human manifestation. Then, as he passes into nirvikalpa samadhi, Arjuna sees all forms disappearing into God, until only a supernatural fire consuming the entire phenomenal world is left.

This supreme vision dazzles Arjuna with the blinding splendor of a thousand suns. Mystics have often described their experiences in this way, in terms of light. In an ancient prayer of the Veda, the poet asks for divine wisdom to dawn in his heart just as the sun rises in the sky. And in the West we have countless testimonies like that of St. Teresa of Avila:

> When the soul looks upon this Divine Sun, the brightness dazzles it. . . . And very often it remains completely blind, absorbed, amazed, and dazzled by all the wonders it sees.

As his vision begins to unfold, Arjuna sees the whole world in the body of Krishna. He sees all things resting in God and all things as divine, and he begins a hymn of praise. He sees Krishna as Vishnu with his traditional weapons, the mace and the discus, and wearing a crown.

As the vision becomes more intense, Arjuna begins to feel afraid. He sees the light of God become a fire that burns to consume all things, as if at the end of time. All the warriors on the battlefield are mortals, and Arjuna sees them slain, burning in the universal fire. All creatures rush to destruction like moths into a flame. God's radiance is both a great light and a burning fire.

Terrified, Arjuna wants to know the identity of this awesome God, who bears no resemblance now to the Krishna he had known as his teacher and friend. In answer to the question, "Who are you?" Krishna's reply is the verse (11:32) that burst into Robert Oppenheimer's mind when he saw the first atomic bomb explode over Trinity in the summer of 1945: "I am become Death, the shatterer of worlds. . . ." But the word *kala* means not just death but time, which eventually devours all creation.

Arjuna is a brave man, worthy of this vision, for he does not lose consciousness or completely break down. He praises Krishna and then asks for forgiveness if he has ever said or done anything to offend the Lord during their long friendship, through mistaking him for a mere human being. Finally, however, the vision is too much for him. Though he experiences the deep peace and joy of samadhi, he is terrified at the same time. He wishes to see the more human face of God.

Krishna grants his desire and returns to his gentle, normal aspect. He tells Arjuna how very difficult it is to see him in his exalted form as the Lord of Yoga, the God of gods. Only pure devotion attains this vision. This is the theme that dominates the remaining chapters of the Gita: it is devotion that is all-important on the spiritual quest.

11 : The Cosmic Vision

ARJUNA:

1 Out of compassion you have taught me the
   supreme mystery of the Self. Through your
2 words my delusion is gone. You have explained the origin and end of every creature,
   O lotus-eyed one, and told me of your own
   supreme, limitless existence.

3 Just as you have described your infinite
   glory, O Lord, now I long to see it. I want to
4 see you as the supreme ruler of creation. O
   Lord, master of yoga, if you think me strong
   enough to behold it, show me your immortal
   Self.

SRI KRISHNA:

5 Behold, Arjuna, a million divine forms, with
6 an infinite variety of color and shape. Behold
   the gods of the natural world, and many more
7 wonders never revealed before. Behold the
   entire cosmos turning within my body, and
   the other things you desire to see.

8 But these things cannot be seen with your
   physical eyes; therefore I give you spiritual
   vision to perceive my majestic power.

SANJAYA :

9   Having spoken these words, Krishna, the
    master of yoga, revealed to Arjuna his most
    exalted, lordly form.

10 He appeared with an infinite number of faces,
    ornamented by heavenly jewels, displaying
    unending miracles and the countless weapons
11 of his power. Clothed in celestial garments
    and covered with garlands, sweet-smelling
    with heavenly fragrances, he showed himself
    as the infinite Lord, the source of all wonders,
    whose face is everywhere.

12 If a thousand suns were to rise in the heavens
    at the same time, the blaze of their light
    would resemble the splendor of that supreme
    spirit.

13 There, within the body of the God of gods,
    Arjuna saw all the manifold forms of the uni-
14 verse united as one. Filled with amazement,
    his hair standing on end in ecstasy, he bowed
    before the Lord with joined palms and spoke
    these words.

ARJUNA:

15 O Lord, I see within your body all the
    gods and every kind of living creature. I see
    Brahma, the Creator, seated on a lotus; I see
    the ancient sages and the celestial serpents.

16 I see infinite mouths and arms, stomachs and
    eyes, and you are embodied in every form. I

see you everywhere, without beginning, middle, or end. You are the Lord of all creation, and the cosmos is your body.

17 You wear a crown and carry a mace and discus; your radiance is blinding and immeasurable. I see you, who are so difficult to behold, shining like a fiery sun blazing in every direction.

18 You are the supreme, changeless Reality, the one thing to be known. You are the refuge of all creation, the immortal spirit, the eternal guardian of eternal dharma.

19 You are without beginning, middle, or end; you touch everything with your infinite power. The sun and moon are your eyes, and your mouth is fire; your radiance warms the cosmos.

20 O Lord, your presence fills the heavens and the earth and reaches in every direction. I see the three worlds trembling before this vision of your wonderful and terrible form.

21 The gods enter your being, some calling out and greeting you in fear. Great saints sing your glory, praying, "May all be well!"

22 The multitudes of gods, demigods, and demons are all overwhelmed by the sight
23 of you. O mighty Lord, at the sight of your

myriad eyes and mouths, arms and legs,
stomachs and fearful teeth, I and the entire
universe shake in terror.

24 O Vishnu, I can see your eyes shining; with
open mouth, you glitter in an array of colors,
and your body touches the sky. I look at you
and my heart trembles; I have lost all courage
and all peace of mind.

25 When I see your mouths with their fearful
teeth, mouths burning like the fires at the end
of time, I forget where I am and I have no
place to go. O Lord, you are the support of
the universe; have mercy on me!

26 I see all the sons of Dhritarashtra; I see Bhishma, Drona, and Karna; I see our warriors and
27 all the kings who are here to fight. All are
   rushing into your awful jaws; I see some of
28 them crushed by your teeth. As rivers flow
   into the ocean, all the warriors of this world
29 are passing into your fiery jaws; all creatures
   rush to their destruction like moths into a
   flame.

30 You lap the worlds into your burning mouths
and swallow them. Filled with your terrible
radiance, O Vishnu, the whole of creation
bursts into flames.

31 Tell me who you are, O Lord of terrible
form. I bow before you; have mercy! I want

to know who you are, you who existed before all creation. Your nature and workings confound me.

SRI KRISHNA:

32 I am time, the destroyer of all; I have come to consume the world. Even without your participation, all the warriors gathered here will die.

33 Therefore arise, Arjuna; conquer your enemies and enjoy the glory of sovereignty. I have already slain all these warriors; you will only be my instrument.

34 Bhishma, Drona, Jayadratha, Karna, and many others are already slain. Kill those whom I have killed. Do not hesitate. Fight in this battle and you will conquer your enemies.

SANJAYA:

35 Having heard these words, Arjuna trembled in fear. With joined palms he bowed before Krishna and addressed him stammering.

ARJUNA:

36 O Krishna, it is right that the world delights and rejoices in your praise, that all the saints and sages bow down to you and all evil flees before you to the far corners of the universe.

37 How could they not worship you, O Lord? You are the eternal spirit, who existed before Brahma the Creator and who will never cease

to be. Lord of the gods, you are the abode
of the universe. Changeless, you are what is
and what is not, and beyond the duality of
existence and nonexistence.

38 You are the first among the gods, the timeless
spirit, the resting place of all beings. You are
the knower and the thing which is known.
You are the final home; with your infinite
form you pervade the cosmos.

39 You are Vayu, god of wind; Yama, god of
death; Agni, god of fire; Varuna, god of
water. You are the moon and the creator
Prajapati, and the great-grandfather of all
creatures. I bow before you and salute you
again and again.

40 You are behind me and in front of me;
I bow to you on every side. Your power is
immeasurable. You pervade everything;
you are everything.

41 Sometimes, because we were friends, I rashly
said, "Oh, Krishna!" "Say, friend!"—casual,
42 careless remarks. Whatever I may have said
lightly, whether we were playing or resting,
alone or in company, sitting together or eating, if it was disrespectful, forgive me for it,
O Krishna. I did not know the greatness of
your nature, unchanging and imperishable.

43 You are the father of the universe, of the animate and the inanimate; you are the object of

all worship, the greatest guru. There is none to equal you in the three worlds. Who can
44 match your power? O gracious Lord, I prostrate myself before you and ask for your blessing. As a father forgives his son, or a friend a friend, or a lover his beloved, so should you forgive me.

45 I rejoice in seeing you as you have never been seen before, yet I am filled with fear by this vision of you as the abode of the universe. Please let me see you again as the shining God
46 of gods. Though you are the embodiment of all creation, let me see you again not with a thousand arms but with four, carrying the mace and discus and wearing a crown.

SRI KRISHNA:

47 Arjuna, through my grace you have been united with me and received this vision of my radiant, universal form, without beginning or end, which no one else has ever seen.

48 Not by knowledge of the Vedas, nor sacrifice, nor charity, nor rituals, nor even by severe asceticism has any other mortal seen what you have seen, O heroic Arjuna.

49 Do not be troubled; do not fear my terrible form. Let your heart be satisfied and your fears dispelled in looking at me as I was before.

SANJAYA:

50 Having spoken these words, the Lord once

again assumed the gentle form of Krishna and consoled his devotee, who had been so afraid.

ARJUNA:

51 O Krishna, now that I have seen your gentle human form my mind is again composed and returned to normal.

SRI KRISHNA:

52 It is extremely difficult to obtain the vision you have had; even the gods long always to
53 see me in this aspect. Neither knowledge of the Vedas, nor austerity, nor charity, nor sac-
54 rifice can bring the vision you have seen. But through unfailing devotion, Arjuna, you can know me, see me, and attain union with me.
55 Whoever makes me the supreme goal of all his work and acts without selfish attachment, who devotes himself to me completely and is free from ill will for any creature, enters into me.

Chapter Twelve

The Way of Love

THIS SHORT chapter focuses upon the supreme importance of devotion and faith in spiritual development. The central idea of this part of the Gita is that love, or personal devotion, is the most powerful motivation in spiritual life.

Certainly the world's great religions would agree with the Gita at this point. All religions allow for a way of devotion, and millions of men and women have found spiritual fulfillment in devotion to Christ, the Buddha, or Mohammed. Hinduism has allowed a place for the path of knowledge as well as the path of devotion; here, however, the Gita stresses the efficacy of devotion.

The Upanishads, the final word on mystic experience uttered by the Vedas, stressed the ultimate reality, the eternal truth behind the ephemeral things of this world. The teachers of the Upanishads told their students to seek knowledge of the Atman, their true Self. The consummation of this knowledge was to know that the Self within was one with Brahman, the ultimate reality pervading all things. This was summed up in the statement *Tat tvam asi,* "You are that"—that imperishable being, that immortal Reality. Brahman, the nameless, formless Godhead, could be known only in the superconscious state.

The Gita backs away from such an approach to religion. For as Krishna says, seeking an eternal, indefinable, hidden Godhead is rather a tall order for the average (or even above average) person. In fact, in this chapter it is said to be beyond the reach of practically all "embodied beings" (*dehavat,* literally "those who have bodies"). Insofar as all creatures do dwell in bodies, is Krishna saying that this path of wisdom is just too "spiritual" for earth's children? In any case, those who identify to a large degree with their physical nature would find the way of knowledge too steep a climb. We can turn to one of the Western followers of this path to see why; this is Dionysius the Areopagite, a Christian monk of probably the fifth century, sounding remarkably like verses 3–4 of this very chapter:

> Then, beyond all distinction between knower and known, the aspirant becomes merged in the nameless, formless Reality, wholly absorbed in That which is beyond all things and in nothing else. . . . Having stilled his intellect and mind, he is united by his highest faculty with That which is beyond all knowing.

Fortunately there is the path of love; for when God is loved in a human aspect, the way is vastly easier. According to the Hindu scriptures, God can be loved as a merciful father, a divine mother, a wise friend, a passionate beloved, or even as a mischievous child.

We might turn to the Christian mystics for help here, for most of them have walked the way of love. The medieval Christian work called *The Cloud of Unknowing* states that love is the sure, safe path to God: "By love He can be gotten and holden, by thought never." In a well-known passage in the New Testament, St. Paul puts love above knowledge and even above miraculous powers: "But I shall give you a more excellent way. . . . Love never faileth. But whether there be prophecies, they shall fail. Whether there be tongues, they shall cease. Whether there be knowledge, it shall vanish away." And St. John of the Cross tells concisely why the vast majority of human beings find it easier to overcome their weaknesses through love of God than through knowledge of him:

> In order to overcome our desires and to renounce all those things, our love and inclination for which are wont to inflame the will that it delights therein, we require a more ardent fire and a nobler love—that of the Bridegroom. . . . if our spiritual nature were not on fire with other and nobler passions, we should never cast off the yoke of the senses.

But such love is often not forthcoming in the struggling soul, even in one like Arjuna. So Krishna says that if Arjuna is not able to focus his devotion, he should learn to do so through the regular practice of meditation. In this the Gita is being practical. Even love and devotion can be cultivated through regular practice; they needn't be regarded as mysterious forces, divine gifts of the spirit.

If even this attempt at regular practice should fail, Krishna is still not ready to let Arjuna off the hook. He should, Krishna says, try working selflessly without desire for the fruits of his labors. But real peace of mind comes only from renunciation. The word *tyaga* here seems to mean renunciation or abandonment of self-will more than anything else. Such self-surrender may be a last resort, but if it is genuine it brings immediate peace.

Verses 13–20 describe the characteristics of the genuine lover of God. Such a saintly person, Krishna points out, is greatly loved and dear to Krishna himself.

12 : *The Way of Love*

1   Of those steadfast devotees who love you and those who seek you as the eternal formless Reality, who are the more established in yoga?

SRI KRISHNA:

2   Those who set their hearts on me and worship me with unfailing devotion and faith are more established in yoga.

3   As for those who seek the transcendental Reality, without name, without form, contemplating the Unmanifested, beyond the
4   reach of thought and of feeling, with their senses subdued and mind serene and striving for the good of all beings, they too will verily come unto me.

5   Yet hazardous and slow is the path to the Unrevealed, difficult for physical man to tread.
6   But they for whom I am the supreme goal, who do all work renouncing self for me and meditate on me with single-hearted devotion,
7   these I will swiftly rescue from the fragment's cycle of birth and death, for their consciousness has entered into me.

8 Still your mind in me, still your intellect in me, and without doubt you will be united
9 with me forever. If you cannot still your mind in me, learn to do so through the regular prac-
10 tice of meditation. If you lack the will for such self-discipline, engage yourself in my work, for selfless service can lead you at last to com-
11 plete fulfillment. If you are unable to do even this, surrender yourself to me, disciplining yourself and renouncing the results of all your actions.

12 Better indeed is knowledge than mechanical practice. Better than knowledge is medita-tion. But better still is surrender of attachment to results, because there follows immediate peace.

13 That one I love who is incapable of ill will, who is friendly and compassionate. Living beyond the reach of *I* and *mine* and of pleasure
14 and pain, patient, contented, self-controlled, firm in faith, with all his heart and all his mind given to me—with such a one I am in love.

15 Not agitating the world or by it agitated, he stands above the sway of elation, competi-tion, and fear: he is my beloved.

16 He is detached, pure, efficient, impartial, never anxious, selfless in all his undertakings; he is my devotee, very dear to me.

17 He is dear to me who runs not after the

pleasant or away from the painful, grieves
not, lusts not, but lets things come and go as
they happen.

18 That devotee who looks upon friend and foe
with equal regard, who is not buoyed up by
praise nor cast down by blame, alike in heat
and cold, pleasure and pain, free from selfish
19 attachments, the same in honor and dishonor,
quiet, ever full, in harmony everywhere, firm
in faith—such a one is dear to me.

20 Those who meditate upon this immortal
dharma as I have declared it, full of faith and
seeking me as life's supreme goal, are truly
my devotees, and my love for them is very
great.

Chapter Thirteen
The Field and the Knower

THIS CHAPTER presents us with two sweeping categories: the "field" and the "knower of the field." To
simplify it somewhat, we may think of the field as the
body and the knower of the field as the Self that resides
in the body. This chapter, then, is about the duality
between "soul and body." This duality is seen as eternal, a basic division of all things—a fundamental concept elaborated in Sankhya philosophy.

We said that the "field" is the body, but this is not
precise enough. The field also includes the mind: in
fact, it comprises all the components of prakriti including the "I"-sense, *ahamkara*—the awareness each of us
has that we are an individual ego, from *aham* "I" and
kara "maker." Ahamkara is the basic awareness of
separateness: that which makes me "I," a being separate from the rest of creation. In this wide sense the
field takes in pretty much everything, except for the
elusive consciousness that "knows" the field. The field
is the object; the knower is the subject. Krishna adds
that he is the hidden knower of the field: that is, the
Self.

This term "field" is a surprisingly modern one, for it
describes what today we might call an extension of the
continuum of mass, energy, time, and space to include
the strata of mind as well—in other words, a field of
forces both physical and mental. Just as physics no
longer regards matter and energy as essentially sepa-

rate, the Gita would not regard matter and mind as separate; they are different aspects of prakriti, the underlying "stuff" of existence.

Another dimension of Krishna's use of the word "field" is brought out by a traditional Hindu anecdote. A wandering *sadhu* or holy man is asked what his work in life is; he replies, "I'm a farmer." When the questioner looks surprised he adds, "This body of mine is my field. I sow good thoughts and actions, and in my body I reap the results." The Buddha explains, "All that we are is the result of what we have thought: it is founded on our thoughts; it is made of our thoughts." What we think, we become, for as Emerson says, the ancestor of every action is a thought. Thus our thoughts, taken together, bear fruit in the actions, decisions, desires, and so forth that shape our lives. In part, the body bears the fruit of what we think insofar as our way of thinking affects our health and safety. But in a larger sense, the whole field of human activity (indeed the whole of prakriti, creation) is also a "field of karma"—where, for example, the global environment is shaped by the sum of what its inhabitants do, which in turn is shaped by how they think. This idea will be picked up and elaborated on in detail in the concluding chapters of the Gita.

Verses 7–11 then describe the person who understands his or her own true nature. This is an attractive picture of the modest, truly wise person who is in control of his or her own life. One implication of these verses is that it is quite an achievement to understand the difference between the field and the Self, the knower. Most people confuse the two, taking the body, mind, and so on to be who they are. In the usual course of events, most people are totally unaware that there is a Self, a consciousness underneath the surface awareness of a separate "I." Verses 12–17 describe the

ultimate underlying reality: Brahman, pure, undifferentiated consciousness, the divine ground of existence.

Verse 19 returns us to the discussion of the basic duality of mind/matter and spirit (Self). Again the technical
terms *prakriti* and *Purusha* are used. Purusha is the
knower and prakriti the field. From the union of these
two all things are born. Both prakṛiti and Purusha are
essential to the creation of the world: nothing could
exist without the spiritual basis of Purusha, and nothing
could develop in a manifest form without the mind and
matter of prakriti.

With its need to think of abstract principles in human
terms, Hinduism embodies these two eternal principles
in the figures of Shiva and Shakti, the divine Father and
Mother. The Gita does not mention these two because it
comes essentially from the Vishnu tradition, but in the
other great stream of the Hindu faith, Shiva is the eternal Spirit, the Absolute, represented as dwelling aloof
on the mountain peak of spiritual peace. Shakti, the
Divine Mother, is his creative partner, and without her,
Shiva could never have created the world. Shakti—she
has many names in her various manifestations—rules in
the realm of birth and death; Shiva, Purusha, lives in the
realm of the immortal. Together the two represent
Brahman, the attributeless Godhead, and the creative
power of the Godhead called maya. Thus it is in the
union of Shiva and Shakti that all things are born.

This chapter emphasizes that the Self, the real knower, is ever uninvolved in the shifting forces that play
over the field. There is no possibility of any soul being
eternally lost, for all beings partake of the immortal,
pure nature of Purusha. We may endure countless eons
of birth and death, but we must finally find our rest in
the eternal spirit. By definition, nothing taking place in
the realm of prakriti can affect Purusha; but the exact

nature of the interaction of these two is a profound mystery.

Verse 32 attempts to explain this mystery by drawing a comparison with *akasha,* the subtlest element recognized by the ancient philosophers. Akasha is space itself. Just as it pervades the cosmos, yet remains pure even in the midst of impure things, so the Self remains completely pure, even though it dwells in all things. Though it seems to live in the land of mortals and to undergo change and death, the real knower in every creature is deathless, "hidden in the heart."

13 : The Field and the Knower

SRI KRISHNA:

1 The body is called a field, Arjuna; he who
knows it is called the Knower of the field.
This is the knowledge of those who know.

2 I am the Knower of the field in everyone,
Arjuna. Knowledge of the field and its
Knower is true knowledge.

3 Listen and I will explain the nature of the field
and how change takes place within it. I will
also describe the Knower of the field and his

4 power. These truths have been sung by great
sages in a variety of ways, and expounded in
precise arguments concerning Brahman.

5 The field, Arjuna, is made up of the following: the five areas of sense perception; the five
elements; the five sense organs and the five
organs of action; the three components of the
mind: *manas, buddhi*, and *ahamkara*; and the
undifferentiated energy from which all these

6 evolved. In this field arise desire and aversion,
pleasure and pain, the body, intelligence, and
will.

7 Those who know truly are free from pride
   and deceit. They are gentle, forgiving, upright, and pure, devoted to their spiritual
   teacher, filled with inner strength, and self-
8 controlled. Detached from sense objects and
   self-will, they have learned the painful lesson
   of separate birth and suffering, old age,
   disease, and death.

9 Free from selfish attachment, they do not get
   compulsively entangled even in home and
   family. They are even-minded through good
10 fortune and bad. Their devotion to me is un-
   divided. Enjoying solitude and not following
11 the crowd, they seek only me. This is true
   knowledge, to seek the Self as the true end
   of wisdom always. To seek anything else is
   ignorance.

12 I will tell you of the wisdom that leads to immortality: the beginningless Brahman, which
   can be called neither being nor nonbeing.

13 It dwells in all, in every hand and foot and
   head, in every mouth and eye and ear in the
14 universe. Without senses itself, it shines
   through the functioning of the senses. Completely independent, it supports all things.
   Beyond the gunas, it enjoys their play.

15 It is both near and far, both within and without every creature; it moves and is unmoving.
16 In its subtlety it is beyond comprehension. It
   is indivisible, yet appears divided in separate

creatures. Know it to be the creator, the preserver, and the destroyer.

17 Dwelling in every heart, it is beyond darkness.
It is called the light of lights, the object and goal
of knowledge, and knowledge itself.

18 I have revealed to you the nature of the field
and the meaning and object of true knowledge.
Those who are devoted to me, knowing these
things, are united with me.

19 Know that prakriti and Purusha are both
without beginning, and that from prakriti come
20 the gunas and all that changes. Prakriti is the
agent, cause, and effect of every action, but
it is Purusha that seems to experience pleasure
and pain.

21 Purusha, resting in prakriti, witnesses the
play of the gunas born of prakriti. But attachment to the gunas leads a person to be born
for good or evil.

22 Within the body the supreme Purusha is called
the witness, approver, supporter, enjoyer, the
supreme Lord, the highest Self.

23 Whoever realizes the true nature of Purusha,
prakriti, and the gunas, whatever path he or
she may follow, is not born separate again.

24 Some realize the Self within them through the
practice of meditation, some by the path of

wisdom, and others by selfless service.

25 Others may not know these paths; but hearing and following the instructions of an illumined teacher, they too go beyond death.

26 Whatever exists, Arjuna, animate or inanimate, is born through the union of the field and its Knower.

27 He alone sees truly who sees the Lord the same in every creature, who sees the Death-
28 less in the hearts of all that die. Seeing the same Lord everywhere, he does not harm himself or others. Thus he attains the supreme goal.

29 They alone see truly who see that all actions are performed by prakriti, while the Self re-
30 mains unmoved. When they see the variety of creation rooted in that unity and growing out of it, they attain fulfillment in Brahman.

31 This supreme Self is without a beginning, undifferentiated, deathless. Though it dwells in the body, Arjuna, it neither acts nor is
32 touched by action. As akasha pervades the cosmos but remains unstained, the Self can never be tainted though it dwells in every creature.

33 As the sun lights up the world, the Self dwelling in the field is the source of all light in the

34 field. Those who, with the eye of wisdom, distinguish the field from its Knower and the way to freedom from the bondage of prakriti, attain the supreme goal.

Chapter Fourteen
The Forces of Evolution

THE LAST chapter gave us the distinction between Purusha and prakriti. This chapter will tell us in more detail about the nature of prakriti—the basis of the world of mind and matter that we find ourselves living in. Here the Gita explains human experience in terms of the three qualities of prakriti, known as *gunas*: *sattva, rajas,* and *tamas*. When the soul attains illumination it goes beyond the confines of prakriti into the spiritual realm of Purusha. But until that happens, the soul must learn to deal with these three all-powerful forces.

No single English word can be given to translate the words *sattva, rajas,* and *tamas*. Sattva is a quality that combines goodness, purity, light, harmony, balance. In terms of evolution, sattva is on the highest level. Rajas is energy—or, on the human level, passion—which can be both good and bad. In personality rajas may express itself in anger, hatred, or greed; but it also provides motivation, the will to act. Rajas is ambitious, which is not altogether a bad thing for the evolution of the soul. It is definitely superior to the third guna, tamas, which combines inertia, sloth, darkness, ignorance, insensitivity. This is the lowest state in terms of evolution; for tamas means a dead stability, where nothing much happens for good or ill. Worse, tamas can mean not just stability but a sliding backwards in the struggle of evolution, where to stand still may mean to be left behind (14:18).

In any given personality or phenomenon all the three gunas are likely to be present. It is the mix of the three that colors our experience. Sattva may be dominant, with an admixture of rajas or tamas. Or perhaps rajas dominates, with a little sattva and a good measure of tamas. Finally, the personality may be basically tamasic, with a few rays of the light of sattva and a little of the heat of rajas. In any case, no mix of the three gunas is stable, for it is the very nature of prakriti to be in constant flux. The gunas are constantly shifting, always changing in intensity.

It is essential that the gunas, even the purity and goodness of sattva, be transcended if the soul is to attain its final peace. For the three gunas are forces that operate within the world of prakriti: in fact, their three strands make up the whole fabric of the phenomenal world. Liberation lies beyond the conditioning of prakriti, in the realm of Purusha. When Arjuna asks Krishna to describe the person who has gone beyond prakriti's net, Krishna replies that such a person is detached from the constant shifting and interaction of the gunas. Identified with the Self, he or she realizes that the gunas and their play are external — even the emotions and thoughts that seem so personal, so interior, are really only the play of prakriti. The thoughts and emotions that disturb ahamkara stop at the gate of the inner Self. The Self abides in the inner chamber of the heart, always at peace, whatever forces of prakriti may storm outside. The illumined man or woman maintains a joyful evenness of mind in happiness and sorrow.

At the end of the chapter, again reminding Arjuna of the power of devotion (*bhakti*), Krishna says that Arjuna can transcend the gunas through steadfast love. If he has devotion and has gone beyond the three gunas, then he will be fit to know Brahman.

14 : The Forces of Evolution

SRI KRISHNA:

1 Let me tell you more about the wisdom that
   transcends all knowledge, through which the
2 saints and sages attained perfection. Those
   who rely on this wisdom will be united with
   me. For them there is neither rebirth nor fear
   of death.

3 My womb is prakriti; in that I place the seed.
4 Thus all created things are born. Everything
   born, Arjuna, comes from the womb of
   prakriti, and I am the seed-giving father.

5 It is the three gunas born of prakriti—sattva,
   rajas, and tamas—that bind the immortal Self
6 to the body. Sattva—pure, luminous, and free
   from sorrow—binds us with attachment to
7 happiness and wisdom. Rajas is passion, arising from selfish desire and attachment. These
8 bind the Self with compulsive action. Tamas,
   born of ignorance, deludes all creatures
   through heedlessness, indolence, and sleep.

9 Sattva binds us to happiness; rajas binds us to
   action. Tamas, distorting our understanding,
   binds us to delusion.

10 Sattva predominates when rajas and tamas
are transformed. Rajas prevails when sattva
is weak and tamas overcome. Tamas prevails
when rajas and sattva are dormant.

11 When sattva predominates, the light of wisdom shines through every gate of the body.
12 When rajas predominates, a person runs about
pursuing selfish and greedy ends, driven by
13 restlessness and desire. When tamas is dominant a person lives in darkness—slothful, confused, and easily infatuated.

14 Those dying in the state of sattva attain the
15 pure worlds of the wise. Those dying in rajas
are reborn among people driven by work. But
those who die in tamas are conceived in the
wombs of the ignorant.

16 The fruit of good deeds is pure and sattvic.
The fruit of rajas is suffering. The fruit of
tamas is ignorance and insensitivity.

17 From sattva comes understanding; from rajas,
greed. But the outcome of tamas is confusion,
infatuation, and ignorance.

18 Those who live in sattva go upwards; those
in rajas remain where they are. But those
immersed in tamas sink downwards.

19 The wise see clearly that all action is the work
of the gunas. Knowing that which is above
the gunas, they enter into union with me.

20 Going beyond the three gunas which form the body, they leave behind the cycle of birth and death, decrepitude and sorrow, and attain to immortality.

ARJUNA:

21 What are the characteristics of those who have gone beyond the gunas, O Lord? How do they act? How have they passed beyond the gunas' hold?

SRI KRISHNA:

22 They are unmoved by the harmony of sattva, the activity of rajas, or the delusion of tamas. They feel no aversion when these forces are active, nor do they crave for them when these forces subside.

23 They remain impartial, undisturbed by the actions of the gunas. Knowing that it is the gunas which act, they abide within themselves and do not vacillate.

24 Established within themselves, they are equal in pleasure and pain, praise and blame, kindness and unkindness. Clay, a rock, and gold
25 are the same to them. Alike in honor and dishonor, alike to friend and foe, they have given up every selfish pursuit. Such are those who have gone beyond the gunas.

26 By serving me with steadfast love, a man or woman goes beyond the gunas. Such a one is fit for union with Brahman. For I am the sup-

port of Brahman, the eternal, the unchanging, the deathless, the everlasting dharma, the source of all joy.

Chapter Fifteen
The Supreme Self

THIS IS a difficult chapter, for it deals essentially with questions of theology. Krishna has described prakriti; now he describes the nature of God. Such questions intrigued the author of the Gita, though they were not his primary concern. This practicality is part of the Gita's appeal: in today's intellectual world, it seems, we have largely lost interest in contemplating questions of theology and philosophy. In Chapter 15, however, we must briefly delve into such mysteries.

Krishna reveals that he transcends not only the world of matter but also the immortal Atman that dwells as the conscious "knower" within all beings. Krishna has said that he is the Atman; but the paradox is that he also transcends the Atman. In this highest aspect Krishna is Ishvara, the cosmic Lord, who abides in his own mystery. The liberated Self enjoys union with Krishna and lives in Krishna's highest home. But the Self does not become Krishna: the immortal soul, even when liberated from its mortal journeying, does not become God.

The chapter opens with the image of an upside-down tree, a world-tree rooted in Brahman which branches out into a manifold creation in this world below. This is said to be an *ashvattha* or pipal tree. Like the banyan, it sends out roots into the air, spreading above and below. The ashvattha is a fig tree and is considered sacred.

As this is a chapter about Krishna's most exalted nature, it is appropriate that his "home," the highest goal of all, is described. It is an abode of light and eternal life. By its very nature, it is beyond the description of human language. Verse 4 uses one of the most elemental and ancient of words for the ultimate reality that defies all description, all human thought: *Tat,* which means simply "that" or "it." Here the Gita personalizes Tat to the extent of giving It a home: *avyayam padam,* the immortal home, the eternal goal. *Pada* also means foot or step, and it is of interest here to recall an ancient myth of the Vedas. According to this myth, at the beginning of time Vishnu took three steps that measured out the entire cosmos. The third and highest step became a heavenly world, the realm of the blessed. In this verse from the Rig Veda (1:154:5), the poet longs to find himself in this home of the god:

> May I go to his blessed world
> Where those who love the gods rejoice;
> For there, truly, is the company of the far-stepping god,
> A fountain of honey in the highest step of Vishnu.

The Gita describes Krishna's home as a realm of light beyond the light of the sun (15:6). Here we might compare the Gita with the Katha Upanishad (5:15):

> There shines not the sun, neither moon nor star,
> Nor flash of lightning, nor fire lit on earth.
> The Self is the light reflected by all.
> He shining, everything shines after him.

Even here, though, we are reminded that Krishna lives not just in this highest realm but also in this world below, where both darkness and light coexist. In his divine mystery he sends fragments of himself to become the inner Self in each creature. In this sense the Self enters the body at conception, dwells in the body, and then departs at death. Krishna is the prana—the breath or vitality—of the body. The ancient scriptures speak of five pranas; here the Gita mentions the two most prominent: the prana by which we breathe and the prana that digests food.

15 : The Supreme Self

1   Sages speak of the immutable ashvattha tree,
    with its taproot above and its branches below.
    On this tree grow the scriptures; seeing their
    source, one knows their essence.

2   Nourished by the gunas, the limbs of this tree
    spread above and below. Sense objects grow
    on the limbs as buds; the roots hanging down
    bind us to action in this world.

3   The true form of this tree—its essence,
    beginning, and end—is not perceived on this
    earth. Cut down this strong-rooted tree with
4   the sharp axe of detachment; then find the
    path which does not come back again. Seek
    That, the First Cause, from which the uni-
    verse came long ago.

5   Not deluded by pride, free from selfish
    attachment and selfish desire, beyond the
    duality of pleasure and pain, ever aware of the
    Self, the wise go forward to that eternal goal.
6   Neither the sun nor the moon nor fire can
    add to that light. This is my supreme abode,

and those who enter there do not return to
separate existence.

7 An eternal part of me enters into the world,
   assuming the powers of action and percep-
8 tion and a mind made of prakriti. When
   the divine Self enters and leaves a body, it
   takes these along as the wind carries a scent
9 from place to place. Using the mind, ears,
   eyes, nose, and the senses of taste and touch,
   the Self enjoys sense objects.

10 The deluded do not see the Self when it leaves
    the body or when it dwells within it. They
    do not see the Self enjoying sense objects or
    acting through the gunas. But they who have
    the eye of wisdom see.

11 Those who strive resolutely on the path of
    yoga see the Self within. The thoughtless,
    who strive imperfectly, do not.

12 The brightness of the sun, which lights up
    the world, the brightness of the moon and
13 of fire—these are my glory. With a drop of
    my energy I enter the earth and support all
    creatures. Through the moon, the vessel of
14 life-giving fluid, I nourish all plants. I enter
    breathing creatures and dwell within as the
    life-giving breath. I am the fire in the stomach
    which digests all food.

15 Entering into every heart, I give the power

to remember and understand; it is I again who take that power away. All the scriptures lead to me; I am their author and their wisdom.

16 In this world there are two orders of being: the perishable, separate creature and the
17 changeless spirit. But beyond these there is another, the supreme Self, the eternal Lord, who enters into the entire cosmos and supports it from within.

18 I am that supreme Self, praised by the scriptures as beyond the changing and the change-
19 less. Those who see in me that supreme Self see truly. They have found the source of all wisdom, Arjuna, and they worship me with all their heart.

20 I have shared this profound truth with you, Arjuna. Those who understand it will attain wisdom; they will have done that which has to be done.

Chapter Sixteen
Two Paths

THIS IS a most unusual chapter, for here the Gita departs from its lofty view of human nature and describes two tendencies among mankind. The higher tendency, the divine, leads to increasing happiness in the course of the soul's evolution, and eventually to its liberation; but there is also a downward tendency leading to suffering and enslavement of the spirit. This chapter is unusual in giving equal, if not in fact more, attention to this dark side of human affairs. Here we get a detailed description of the divine qualities that liberate and the "demonic" qualities that enslave (16:5).

Usually upbeat, Krishna here changes his tone and describes the sinful person, the individual of a demonic sort, with great vigor—and it seems he knows what he is talking about. But first he assures Arjuna that he is of the divine sort, so he shouldn't get too nervous.

The "demonic" personality is basically atheistic. For such people life does not originate in God or a divine reality but is grounded in biology, in sexual desire and the sex act. Taking a low view of human nature, such people cause suffering to themselves as well as others. They are arrogant and have many insatiable selfish desires, and they do not hesitate to do anything that will get them what they want. Krishna grants that they may have a good time, getting wealthy and enjoying themselves, but their destination is hell—a hell of their own making, often in this very life, as the karma of their ways of thinking and behaving bears fruit.

One of the least likable characteristics of "demonic" personalities is their sense of self-importance. They like to give gifts ostentatiously and offer ritual sacrifices; this seems to legitimize their wealth and makes them feel respectable and esteemed. They like being generous if it will make them look good.

Krishna does not disguise his dislike for cruel people. He tells Arjuna that he arranges for them to be born again and again in a harsh world. Such souls cannot seem to purify their sinful hearts; repeating the same selfish ways, they sink lower and lower. This is a very bleak picture, which the Gita dwells on only in this chapter. But even here, amidst the gloom and doom, Krishna will not say that such a soul is eternally damned. It may be that such a sinful creature condemns himself to birth after birth in harsh, unfavorable circumstances, sinking into more and more hellish states of mind; but the cycle goes on, the choice to change direction is always open, and the Atman itself can never be stained. This forced exposure to harsh circumstances is necessary if such an incorrigibly selfish and cruel personality is to learn to be sensitive to suffering and not go on causing it to others—the first step in its regeneration.

Lust, anger, and greed are the three doors to hell that Arjuna must at all costs not enter. If anyone can pass by these three tempting doors and not enter them, that is the best: the person who enters will not only fail to reach life's final goal, but will not even achieve lasting happiness and prosperity.

In Sanskrit this chapter is called the "Way of Divine and Demonic Destinies." The words *deva,* god, and *asura,* demon, are not to be taken too literally here. The Hindu scriptures often tell stories of the battles between the gods and the demons; thus they dramatize the struggle between good and evil in the world. Probably no divine character from Hindu myth escapes a challenge from some demon. Usually the god or goddess is victorious; but often the demon will win a battle or two, though not the final victory. Krishna has a long battle record, celebrated by epithets like Madhusudana, "slayer of the demon Madhu." Rama, another incarnation of Vishnu, had to confront and kill Ravana. The stories go on. The gods never seem to rest for long: there is always a new challenge to their authority, a new source of malignant evil to be destroyed.

The Mahabharata and the Gita, however, do not dwell on these mythical battles. Here the interest is more frankly human, and when Krishna discusses the "divine" and "demonic" qualities, he speaks not of gods and demons but of human good and evil.

16 : Two Paths

1   Be fearless and pure; never waver in your determination or your dedication to the spiritual life. Give freely. Be self-controlled, sincere, truthful, loving, and full of the desire to serve. Realize the truth of the scriptures; learn to be

2   detached and to take joy in renunciation. Do not get angry or harm any living creature, but be compassionate and gentle; show good will

3   to all. Cultivate vigor, patience, will, purity; avoid malice and pride. Then, Arjuna, you will achieve your divine destiny.

4   Other qualities, Arjuna, make a person more and more inhuman: hypocrisy, arrogance, conceit, anger, cruelty, ignorance.

5   The divine qualities lead to freedom; the demonic, to bondage. But do not grieve, Arjuna; you were born with divine attributes.

6   Some people have divine tendencies, others demonic. I have described the divine at length, Arjuna; now listen while I describe the demonic.

7   The demonic do things they should avoid and
    avoid the things they should do. They have
    no sense of uprightness, purity, or truth.

8   "There is no God," they say, "no truth, no
    spiritual law, no moral order. The basis of life
9   is sex; what else can it be?" Holding such dis-
    torted views, possessing scant discrimination,
    they become enemies of the world, causing
    suffering and destruction.

10 Hypocritical, proud, and arrogant, living in
    delusion and clinging to deluded ideas, insatia-
    ble in their desires, they pursue their unclean
11 ends. Although burdened with fears that end
    only with death, they still maintain with com-
    plete assurance, "Gratification of lust is the
    highest that life can offer."

12 Bound on all sides by scheming and anxiety,
    driven by anger and greed, they amass by any
    means they can a hoard of money for the
    satisfaction of their cravings.

13 "I got this today," they say; "tomorrow I
    shall get that. This wealth is mine, and that
14 will be mine too. I have destroyed my ene-
    mies. I shall destroy others too! Am I not like
    God? I enjoy what I want. I am successful. I
15 am powerful. I am happy. I am rich and well-
    born. Who is equal to me? I will perform sac-
    rifices and give gifts, and rejoice in my own
    generosity." This is how they go on, deluded

16 by ignorance. Bound by their greed and entangled in a web of delusion, whirled about
by a fragmented mind, they fall into a dark
hell.

17 Self-important, obstinate, swept away by the
pride of wealth, they ostentatiously perform
sacrifices without any regard for their pur-
18 pose. Egotistical, violent, arrogant, lustful,
angry, envious of everyone, they abuse my
presence within their own bodies and in the
bodies of others.

19 Life after life I cast those who are malicious,
hateful, cruel, and degraded into the wombs
20 of those with similar demonic natures. Birth
after birth they find themselves with demonic
tendencies. Degraded in this way, Arjuna,
they fail to reach me and fall lower still.

21 There are three gates to this self-destructive
hell: lust, anger, and greed. Renounce these
22 three. Those who escape from these three
gates of darkness, Arjuna, seek what is best
23 and attain life's supreme goal. Others dis-
regard the teachings of the scriptures. Driven
by selfish desire, they miss the goal of life,
miss even happiness and success.

24 Therefore let the scriptures be your guide in
what to do and what not to do. Understand
their teachings; then act in accordance with
them.

Chapter Seventeen
The Power of Faith

AT THE END of the last chapter, Krishna told Arjuna to look to the scriptures to guide his actions, so that he can avoid the lower road that leads backwards to a less evolved state. Now Arjuna wants to know about those who do not follow the orthodox way set down in the scriptures, but who nevertheless offer some kind of worship with faith in their hearts.

In reply Krishna goes into greater detail about the three gunas—sattva, rajas, and tamas. He also stresses the importance of *shraddha* or faith. This is a difficult word. "Faith" is not an adequate translation, and the etymology of the word is obscure; it probably has an underlying meaning of "what is held in the heart." We might say that our shraddha is the sum total of our values, what we really hold to be important in our lives. Every human being, Krishna says, is *shraddha-maya,* "made up of faith"—as the Bible puts it, as we think in our heart, so we are.

Here, as elsewhere in the Gita, shraddha is a positive quality. It is good to have faith; yet faith can be of different kinds, different qualities. Sattvic faith is the most evolved, the most pure. Rajasic faith is dynamic, evolving, yet tainted with selfish motives. Tamasic faith founders in a spiritual quagmire.

To illustrate this, Krishna tells Arjuna that sattvic people worship the devas—the gods of heaven, of light. The rajasic worship *yaksha*s and *rakshasa*s. The yakshas are servants of the god of wealth; rakshasas are power-ful, fearsome spirits driven by the lust for power and pleasure. Finally, tamasic people worship the spirits of the dead and ghosts.

In a practical digression, Krishna describes the differ-ent kinds of food liked by the sattvic, the rajasic, and the tamasic. Then he applies the three gunas to the act of worship and sacrifice or selfless service (*yajna*).

In verses 14–16, Krishna turns to the important ques-tion of *tapas* or *sadhana*, the disciplines undergone for the sake of spiritual growth. The Gita holds that no lasting progress is possible on the spiritual path without a great deal of self-discipline. The root of the word *tapas* is *tap,* which means to be hot or to suffer pain; and in fact *tapas* can also mean heat or suffering. The connection is that when certain spiritual practices are mastered, they create a feeling of heat in the body, which is a sign of increased spiritual potency. Tapas also refers to the power gained through spiritual austerity. Krishna dis-pels the mistaken belief that tapas means mortifying or torturing the body, and points out that spiritual disci-plines can be sattvic, rajasic, or tamasic. The sattvic kind of tapas is offered for a truly spiritual goal; rajas, as usual, performs tapas to gain a selfish end, probably the admiration of others. Deluded by tamas, a person will undergo painful, foolish practices to try to gain power over, or even to injure, others. This may be a reference to black magic.

Changing course for a moment, Krishna discusses the mantram *Om Tat Sat. Om* is the most ancient of Hindu mantrams; it is the sacred syllable that is Brah-man, the cosmic sound heard in the depths of medita-tion. *Tat,* as mentioned earlier, is "That," the supreme reality beyond what language can describe or thought can think. And *sat* means both "that which is" and "that which is good." The mantram *Om Tat Sat* affirms that only the good really exists; the opposite word, *asat,* implies that evil is transient and therefore is not ultimately real.

Krishna concludes in the last verse that no act or intention can add to spiritual growth if it is "faithless." An act done without shraddha is *asat*, unreal; it cannot have meaning either in this world or the next.

17 : The Power of Faith

1   O Krishna, what is the state of those who dis-
regard the scriptures but still worship with
faith? Do they act from sattva, rajas, or tamas?

SRI KRISHNA:

2   Every creature is born with faith of some
kind, either sattvic, rajasic, or tamasic. Listen,
and I will describe each to you.

3   Our faith conforms to our nature, Arjuna.
Human nature is made of faith. Indeed, a
person is his faith.

4   Those who are sattvic worship the forms of
God; those who are rajasic worship power
and wealth. Those who are tamasic worship
5   spirits and ghosts. Some invent harsh pen-
ances. Motivated by hypocrisy and egotism,
6   they torture their innocent bodies and me
who dwells within. Blinded by their strength
and passion, they act and think like demons.

7   The three kinds of faith express themselves in
the habits of those who hold them: in the food
they like, the work they do, the disciplines

they practice, the gifts they give. Listen, and I
will describe their different ways.

8   Sattvic people enjoy food that is mild, tasty,
    substantial, agreeable, and nourishing, food
    that promotes health, strength, cheerfulness,
9   and longevity. Rajasic people like food that is
    salty or bitter, hot, sour, or spicy—food that
    promotes pain, discomfort, and disease.
10 Tamasic people like overcooked, stale, left-
    over, and impure food, food that has lost its
    taste and nutritional value.

11 The sattvic perform sacrifices with their entire
    mind fixed on the purpose of the sacrifice.
    Without thought of reward, they follow the
12 teachings of the scriptures. The rajasic per-
    form sacrifices for the sake of show and the
13 good it will bring them. The tamasic perform
    sacrifices ignoring both the letter and the
    spirit. They omit the proper prayers, the
    proper offerings, the proper food, and the
    proper faith.

14 To offer service to the gods, to the good, to
    the wise, and to your spiritual teacher; purity,
    honesty, continence, and nonviolence: these
15 are the disciplines of the body. To offer sooth-
    ing words, to speak truly, kindly, and helpful-
    ly, and to study the scriptures: these are the
16 disciplines of speech. Calmness, gentleness,
    silence, self-restraint, and purity: these are the
    disciplines of the mind.

17 When these three levels of self-discipline are
   practiced without attachment to the results,
   but in a spirit of great faith, the sages call this
18 practice sattvic. Disciplines practiced in order
   to gain respect, honor, or admiration are
   rajasic; they are undependable and transitory
19 in their effects. Disciplines practiced to gain
   power over others, or in the confused belief
   that to torture oneself is spiritual, are tamasic.

20 Giving simply because it is right to give,
   without thought of return, at a proper time,
   in proper circumstances, and to a worthy per-
21 son, is sattvic giving. Giving with regrets or in
   the expectation of receiving some favor or of
22 getting something in return is rajasic. Giving
   at an inappropriate time, in inappropriate
   circumstances, and to an unworthy person,
   without affection or respect, is tamasic.

23 *Om Tat Sat*: these three words represent
   Brahman, from which come priests and
24 scriptures and sacrifice. Those who follow the
   Vedas, therefore, always repeat the word *Om*
   when offering sacrifices, performing spiritual
25 disciplines, or giving gifts. Those seeking
   liberation and not any personal benefit add
   the word *Tat* when performing these acts
26 of worship, discipline, and charity. *Sat*
   means "that which is"; it also indicates goodness. Therefore it is used to describe a worthy
   deed.

27 To be steadfast in self-sacrifice, self-discipline, and giving is *sat*. To act in accordance with
28 these three is *sat* as well. But to engage in sacrifice, self-discipline, and giving without good faith is *asat,* without worth or goodness, either in this life or in the next.

Chapter Eighteen
Freedom & Renunciation

THIS FINAL CHAPTER of the Gita roams over many subjects, beginning with a discussion of the merits of renunciation versus the life of personally involved action. To begin with, Arjuna asks about two words commonly used for renunciation in Sanskrit, *sannyasa* and *tyaga*. Both words come from roots meaning to give up or abandon. *Sannyasa* acquired the specialized meaning of giving up ordinary life to live the austere, wandering life of a homeless pilgrim. A *sannyasi* is a monk: he does not participate in family life; he has detached himself from society. In a sense, he has withdrawn from life. Krishna does not recommend this kind of renunciation. In fact, he says it is impossible for anyone to "give up" in this way, for as long as we have a body, we have to do a certain amount of work just to maintain it. Krishna does not advise dropping out of life, and the Gita is primarily aimed at people who live "in the world" yet desire genuine spiritual fulfillment.

The kind of renunciation Krishna recommends is *tyaga,* where it is not activity but selfish desire for the rewards of action—of work, of life—that is to be renounced. Arjuna is advised to fulfill all his responsibilities, but without a selfish motive. In particular, he should not give up the three great virtuous works—sacrifice, giving, and spiritual disciplines.

Having made plain to Arjuna that renunciation is

essential, Krishna goes on to explain that renunciation can be of three kinds, depending upon the guna that dominates the individual's personality. As may be expected, rajasic and tamasic renunciation leave something to be desired.

Many times Krishna has said that renunciation of the fruits of work is essential. Perhaps the verse in Chapter 2 said it best—that we have control over our work and actions, but we have no command of the results. The word *karma-phala-tyaga* appears again and again, and the literal translation is "renunciation of the fruits of action." In this final chapter, literally "The Freedom [moksha] That Comes from Renunciation," Krishna sums up his teaching that in work, in life, one must not be driven by a selfish desire for any kind of reward, for such compulsive work can only stunt full spiritual development. In addition, Krishna points out, when a person acts out of selfish attachment, he must fully partake of the result, the karma, of every thought, word, and deed; and although these results may be what was desired, they may also be something not desired at all, or a little of both (18:12). In this life you can never be sure that things will turn out as planned.

In verse 13 the Sankhya philosophy is again mentioned. Scholars believe that at the time the Gita was composed the Sankhya school was at an early stage of development, yet even here we see the characteristic method of thorough categorizing. Using the Sankhya categories of the three gunas, Krishna goes on to give more detail about work, which is of three kinds—sattvic, rajasic, and tamasic. Similarly, the doer of the work is shown to be dominated by one of these all-pervasive qualities. In a very interesting passage Krishna talks of three kinds of happiness—a practical application of the abstract theories of Sankhya (18:37–39).

Pursuing the world of work, and how it contributes

to spiritual growth, the Gita gives a short explanation of caste in this chapter. The Gita for the most part is not especially interested in caste—the social hierarchy of Hindu society—but we do find a short explanation here. The *sannyasi,* the renouncing monk, has left society and therefore belongs to no caste, but Krishna does not point out that course to Arjuna. Rather, he wants Arjuna to lead an active life. Basically, Krishna tells him that devotion to his own duty is best. It is better to do one's own work, even if imperfectly, than to try to take on some other work. The work proper to each of the four castes is then described. In general, the Gita takes a fairly liberal view of caste, and it would be wrong to interpret this chapter as supporting a very rigid caste system.

The final part of this chapter, verses 50 and following, give a picture of the person who has attained *siddhi*—success or perfection—in the spiritual life and who goes on to union with Brahman.

In verse 61 Krishna returns to a favorite topic—the Lord dwelling in the hearts of all beings. But here he adds a startling revelation: the Lord dwells in all, yet he "whirls them around" through maya as if they were toys mounted on a machine. Having jarred Arjuna with this amazing image, Krishna reassures him that he can escape from the machine, the wheel of time, through devotion to God. If he wholeheartedly takes refuge in the Lord, then through Krishna's grace he will find peace.

As his all but final word, Krishna reminds Arjuna that he holds him very dear. Through devotion to him, Arjuna will be able to find his way, and he should not forget that Krishna feels deep love for him too.

The relationship between the teacher and student is given a parting word, partially of warning. Krishna does not want these profound truths told to anyone who is not ready. Anyone lacking devotion or self-control, who does not want to hear spiritual instruction or who scoffs at it, should not be accepted as a student. The sacred act of giving spiritual instruction cannot be undertaken lightly. It is the highest work, and the man or woman who does it is most dear to Krishna.

Finally, Krishna asks Arjuna if he has understood. Arjuna says yes, his conflicts are over; he is ready to follow Krishna's instructions. This concludes the dialogue between Krishna and Arjuna and the instruction of the Gita proper. Sanjaya, who has been narrating the poem to blind king Dhritarashtra, adds a few final verses of benediction. He has "seen" this dialogue through his mystic vision, granted by the grace of Vyasa. Just recalling this wonderful conversation makes his hair stand on end in ecstasy, and when he remembers Krishna's wonderful beauty, his joy is boundless.

18 : *Freedom & Renunciation*

1 O Krishna, destroyer of evil, please explain to
me sannyasa and tyaga and how one kind of
renunciation differs from another.

SRI KRISHNA:

2 To refrain from selfish acts is one kind of
renunciation, called sannyasa; to renounce
the fruit of action is another, called tyaga.

3 Among the wise, some say that all action
should be renounced as evil. Others say that
certain kinds of action—self-sacrifice, giving,
4 and self-discipline—should be continued. Listen, Arjuna, and I will explain three kinds of
tyaga and my conclusions concerning them.

5 Self-sacrifice, giving, and self-discipline
should not be renounced, for they purify the
6 thoughtful. Yet even these, Arjuna, should be
performed without desire for selfish rewards.
This is essential.

7 To renounce one's responsibilities is not
fitting. The wise call such deluded renuncia-
8 tion tamasic. To avoid action from fear of dif-

ficulty or physical discomfort is rajasic. There
9 is no reward in such renunciation. But to
fulfill your responsibilities knowing that they
are obligatory, while at the same time desiring
nothing for yourself—this is sattvic renuncia-
10 tion. Those endowed with sattva clearly
understand the meaning of renunciation and
do not waver. They are not intimidated by
unpleasant work, nor do they seek a job
because it is pleasant.

11 As long as one has a body, one cannot renounce action altogether. True renunciation
is giving up all desire for personal reward.
12 Those who are attached to personal reward
will reap the consequences of their actions:
some pleasant, some unpleasant, some mixed.
But those who renounce every desire for personal reward go beyond the reach of karma.

13 Listen, Arjuna, and I will explain the five
elements necessary for the accomplishment
of every action, as taught by the wisdom of
14 Sankhya. The body, the means, the ego, the
performance of the act, and the divine will:
15 these are the five factors in all actions, right
or wrong, in thought, word, or deed.

16 Those who do not understand this think of
themselves as separate agents. With their
crude intellects they fail to see the truth.
17 The person who is free from ego, who has
attained purity of heart, though he slays these

people, he does not slay and is not bound by
his action.

18 Knowledge, the thing to be known, and
the knower: these three promote action. The
means, the act itself, and the doer: these three
19 are the totality of action. Knowledge, action,
and the doer can be described according to the
gunas. Listen, and I will explain their distinctions to you.

20 Sattvic knowledge sees the one indestructible Being in all beings, the unity underlying
21 the multiplicity of creation. Rajasic knowledge sees all things and creatures as separate
22 and distinct. Tamasic knowledge, lacking
any sense of perspective, sees one small
part and mistakes it for the whole.

23 Work performed to fulfill one's obligations,
without thought of personal reward or of
whether the job is pleasant or unpleasant, is
24 sattvic. Work prompted by selfish desire or
25 self-will, full of stress, is rajasic. Work that is
undertaken blindly, without any considera-
tion of consequences, waste, injury to others,
or one's own capacities, is tamasic.

26 A sattvic worker is free from egotism and
selfish attachments, full of enthusiasm and
27 fortitude in success and failure alike. A rajasic
worker has strong personal desires and craves
rewards for his actions. Covetous, impure,

and destructive, he is easily swept away by
28 fortune, good or bad. The tamasic worker is
undisciplined, vulgar, stubborn, deceitful,
dishonest, and lazy. He is easily depressed and
prone to procrastination.

29 Listen, Arjuna, as I describe the three types of
understanding and will.

30 To know when to act and when to refrain
from action, what is right action and what
is wrong, what brings security and what insecurity, what brings freedom and what bondage: these are the signs of a sattvic intellect.

31 The rajasic intellect confuses right and wrong
actions, and cannot distinguish what is to be
32 done from what should not be done. The
tamasic intellect is shrouded in darkness,
utterly reversing right and wrong wherever
it turns.

33 The sattvic will, developed through meditation, keeps prana, mind, and senses in vital
34 harmony. The rajasic will, conditioned by
selfish desire, pursues wealth, pleasure, and
35 respectability. The tamasic will shows itself
in obstinate ignorance, sloth, fear, grief,
depression, and conceit.

36 Now listen, Arjuna: there are also three kinds
of happiness. By sustained effort, one comes
to the end of sorrow.

37 That which seems like poison at first, but tastes like nectar in the end—this is the joy of sattva, born of a mind at peace with itself.

38 Pleasure from the senses seems like nectar at first, but it is bitter as poison in the end. This is the kind of happiness that comes to the

39 rajasic. Those who are tamasic draw their pleasures from sleep, indolence, and intoxication. Both in the beginning and in the end, this happiness is a delusion.

40 No creature, whether born on earth or among the gods in heaven, is free from the

41 conditioning of the three gunas. The different responsibilities found in the social order—distinguishing brahmin, kshatriya, vaishya, and shudra—have their roots in this conditioning.

42 The responsibilities to which a brahmin is born, based on his nature, are self-control, tranquility, purity of heart, patience, humility, learning, austerity, wisdom, and faith.

43 The qualities of a kshatriya, based on his nature, are courage, strength, fortitude, dexterity, generosity, leadership, and the

44 firm resolve never to retreat from battle. The occupations suitable for a vaishya are agriculture, dairying, and trade. The proper work of a shudra is service.

45 By devotion to one's own particular duty, everyone can attain perfection. Let me tell

46 you how. By performing his own work, one

worships the Creator who dwells in every
creature. Such worship brings that person to
fulfillment.

47 It is better to perform one's own duties imperfectly than to master the duties of another.
By fulfilling the obligations he is born with, a
48 person never comes to grief. No one should
abandon duties because he sees defects in
them. Every action, every activity, is surrounded by defects as a fire is surrounded by
smoke.

49 He who is free from selfish attachments, who
has mastered himself and his passions, attains
the supreme perfection of freedom from ac-
50 tion. Listen and I shall explain now, Arjuna,
how one who has attained perfection also
attains Brahman, the supreme consummation
of wisdom.

51 Unerring in his discrimination, sovereign of
his senses and passions, free from the clamor
52 of likes and dislikes, he leads a simple, self-
reliant life based on meditation, controlling
his speech, body, and mind.

53 Free from self-will, aggressiveness, arrogance, anger, and the lust to possess people or
things, he is at peace with himself and others
54 and enters into the unitive state. United with
Brahman, ever joyful, beyond the reach of desire and sorrow, he has equal regard for every
living creature and attains supreme devotion

55 to me. By loving me he comes to know me
truly; then he knows my glory and enters
56 into my boundless being. All his acts are
performed in my service, and through my
grace he wins eternal life.

57 Make every act an offering to me; regard me
as your only protector. Relying on interior
58 discipline, meditate on me always. Remembering me, you shall overcome all difficulties
through my grace. But if you will not heed
me in your self-will, nothing will avail you.

59 If you egotistically say, "I will not fight this
battle," your resolve will be useless; your
60 own nature will drive you into it. Your own
karma, born of your own nature, will drive
you to do even that which you do not wish
to do, because of your delusion.

61 The Lord dwells in the hearts of all creatures
and whirls them round upon the wheel of
62 maya. Run to him for refuge with all your
strength, and peace profound will be yours
through his grace.

63 I give you these precious words of wisdom;
reflect on them and then do as you choose.
64 These are the last words I shall speak to you,
dear one, for your spiritual fulfillment. You
are very dear to me.

65 Be aware of me always, adore me, make

every act an offering to me, and you shall
come to me; this I promise; for you are dear
66 to me. Abandon all supports and look to me
for protection. I shall purify you from the
sins of the past; do not grieve.

67 Do not share this wisdom with anyone who
lacks in devotion or self-control, lacks the de-
68 sire to learn, or scoffs at me. Those who teach
this supreme mystery of the Gita to all who
love me perform the greatest act of love; they
69 will come to me without doubt. No one can
render me more devoted service; no one on
earth can be more dear to me.

70 Those who meditate on these holy words
71 worship me with wisdom and devotion. Even
those who listen to them with faith, free from
doubts, will find a happier world where good
people dwell.

72 Have you listened with attention? Are you
now free from your doubts and confusion?

ARJUNA:

73 You have dispelled my doubts and delusions,
and I understand through your grace. My
faith is firm now, and I will do your will.

SANJAYA:

74 This is the dialogue I heard between Krishna,
the son of Vasudeva, and Arjuna, the great-
hearted son of Pritha. The wonder of it makes
75 my hair stand on end! Through Vyasa's grace,

I have heard the supreme secret of spiritual union directly from the Lord of Yoga, Krishna himself.

76 Whenever I remember these wonderful, holy words between Krishna and Arjuna, I
77 am filled with joy. And when I remember the breathtaking form of Krishna, I am filled with wonder and my joy overflows.

78 Wherever the divine Krishna and the mighty Arjuna are, there will be prosperity, victory, happiness, and sound judgment. Of this I am sure!

Notes

1 The phrase "on the field of dharma" (*dharma-kshetre*) gives a hint that the battle is to be an allegorical one, a fight of dharma, justice, against adharma, evil. The battle takes place not only at Kurukshetra, the "field of the Kurus," but also on the elusive "field of dharma," the spiritual realm where all moral struggles are waged.

40–44 These verses are particularly difficult to translate, because they revolve around the complex word *dharma*: law, justice, or simply something's inner nature. To try to capture the word in English we might say "God's law" or "eternal truth." Dharma is divinely given; it is the force that holds things together in a unity, the center that must hold if all is to go well. The opposite of dharma is *adharma*: evil, injustice, chaos. In these verses Arjuna gives expression to his fears of a coming chaos, an evil world where good people will be confused and violated. "Sense of unity" here translates *dharma*; the phrase "loses its sense of unity" would be more literally translated as "is overcome by adharma."

The translation speaks in a general way of the chaos that overcomes society when dharma is weak—when ancient spiritual truths are ignored. Thus *varna-samkara,* literally "confusion of caste," is more meaningful as "society [is] plunged into

215

chaos." The subject here is not the observance of caste restrictions, but the essential cohesion of the social fabric.

42 The Sanskrit refers to the ancient *pinda* rites that offer homage to dead ancestors. These rites maintained the traditions of the family by respecting and worshipping those who had gone before. Again, the rather liberal rendering "the spiritual evolution begun by our ancestors" seems preferable to a narrower translation.

CHAPTER TWO

17 *Tat,* "that," is an ancient name for Brahman, the supreme reality. Brahman is neither masculine nor feminine; in fact, it has no attributes at all. It is impossible to describe Brahman in words, so it is simply pointed to: *tat*.

72 The state of immortality is *brahma-nirvana,* "the nirvana that is Brahman." This is the state of release or liberation, union with the divine ground of existence. The word *nirvana* comes from the Sanskrit root *va* "to blow" with the prefix *nir* "out"; it means "to extinguish," as a fire is said to be "blown out." Thus it indicates the extinction of the old, limited personality. By adding the word *brahman,* complete union with the universal Godhead is indicated. *Brahma-nirvana* then means the mystic state of extinction of self in the union with God. *Nirvana* is a Buddhist term as well, and Buddhist definitions have generally received more attention in the English-speaking world. Because of the austere nature of Buddhist discourse, some misconceptions are unfortunately current about this rather esoteric concept. Nirvana is wrongly presented as a kind of empty nothingness, even a spiritual death. We get exactly the opposite impression if we approach the

Hindus and Buddhists themselves. It is true there is much talk of extinguishing the petty ego and going beyond self-will, but this is just to say that it is necessary to jettison the limited, weak personality—the mask that hides the creative, wise, loving Self underneath. This "death" of the old man to make way for the new is one purpose of spiritual disciplines. It can be painful, but the death of the old man does not lead to annihilation but to a spiritual rebirth.

CHAPTER THREE

9 Here and later *yajna* is translated as "selfless work" or "selfless service." The literal meaning is sacrifice: essentially, self-sacrifice, giving up something one greatly values for the sake of a higher purpose. Some translators give a very narrow translation of *yajna* as a ritualistic sacrifice, but this is inaccurate. The Gita is not at all concerned with ritual religion, and in fact deprecates it quite a few times.

39 *Kama* can be translated as selfish desire or pleasure, and often carries a connotation of sensual desire or sexual passion. It means essentially a personal desire for ease or pleasure, not "desire" of a more altruistic kind.

CHAPTER FOUR

37 This is a well-known verse. The meanings of *karma* are complex, but the verse is widely taken to mean that true knowledge destroys the effects of past errors, which generate further karma. When consciousness is unified and illumined, one is released from the bondage of karma.

CHAPTER FIVE

6 *Yoga* has many meanings in the Gita, some of which are discussed in our introductions. Here *yoga* is

translated as "action" and "selfless service" because a contrast is being made between Sankhya and yoga: that is, between philosophical explanation and the actual practice of the spiritual life.

9 The word for "senses" in Sanskrit is *indriya,* literally "faculty" or "power." The indriyas are not only the five faculties of perception (seeing, hearing, touching, smelling, and tasting) but also those of action, whose organs are the hands, the feet, the tongue, and the organs of excretion and reproduction.

13 "The city of nine gates" is the body. The gates are the two eyes, the two nostrils, the two ears, the mouth, and the organs of excretion and reproduction. In some lists these gates are expanded to eleven by adding the navel and the *brahmarandhra* or sagittal suture, the opening at the top of the skull.

27–28 The area "of spiritual consciousness between the eyebrows" is one of the seven centers of awareness or *chakra*s described in yoga literature. These seven chakras, though not physical, are said to lie along a channel for awakened spiritual energy (*kundalini*) that corresponds with the spine; the chakras are located at the level of the anus, sex organs, stomach, heart, throat, eyebrows, and the top of the head. Kundalini circulates among these centers, but it is usually confined to the lowest three chakras, corresponding to the main preoccupations of life on the physical level. In yogic concentration the vital energy (kundalini) rises; samadhi is said to take place when it reaches the chakras at the brow or head.

CHAPTER SIX

11 This describes the traditional seat used for meditation. The Gita is not concerned with the outer forms

of the spiritual life, but here we do get a mention of the grass and deerskin used by the ancient sages. Perhaps the point is that they used what was available in their forest retreats, and that the seat should be what Patanjali calls *sukhasana*: comfortable enough to forget about your body, not so comfortable that you fall asleep.

14 "All actions dedicated to Brahman" is a literal translation of the Sanskrit word *brahmacharya,* a life of self-control and sense restraint.

CHAPTER SEVEN

16 *Artharthi* has given translators some difficulties. "Those who desire to achieve their purpose" captures the basic meaning of the word. *Artha* is goal or purpose; the second word of the compound, *arthi,* means "one who has a goal." So *artharthi* probably refers to those who take to the spiritual life with a particular purpose in view. *Artha* also means wealth or worldly goods, but to translate this phrase as "those who desire wealth" would go against the entire tenor of the Gita.

23 "The gods" here are the *deva*s, the lower, celestial deities such as Indra.

30 These obscure terms (*adhibhuta, adhidaiva,* and *adhiyajna*) are taken up in the next chapter.

CHAPTER EIGHT

6 Whatever is the content of the mind at the moment of death determines the direction of the soul's rebirth. The implication is that whatever has been the bedrock of consciousness during life will be remembered at the time of death and lead the soul on to fulfill that desire in the next life.

9–10 The eyebrow center is discussed in the note to 5:27–28.

CHAPTER NINE

5 *Yoga* here means "mysterious power." This is yet another meaning attached to the word *yoga,* for those who practiced yoga were sometimes thought of as concealing within themselves extraordinary powers developed through their disciplines. The folklore of India relates many stories about mysterious holy men who have strange, divine powers.

Krishna speaks here of his *yoga aishvaram,* his mysterious and majestic power. *Ishvara* means "lord" and *aishvaram* "lordly": Krishna's yoga is something he uses as Ishvara, the Lord of the world. Now he begins to show Arjuna something of the nature of the mystery.

17 Rig, Yajur, and Sama are the principal Vedas, the ancient scriptures that are Hinduism's orthodox authority.

20–21 These verses repeat the idea that heaven itself is an impermanent state. After exhausting the store of their good karma, the blessed souls in heaven must be reborn on earth. Only the liberated soul, the one who has found union with Krishna or *brahmanirvana,* escapes the round of rebirth and death as a separate, mortal creature.

CHAPTER TEN

This chapter contains many Sanskrit names, which are briefly identified in the Glossary (see p.225).

18 *Amrita,* "immortal," comes from *a* "not" and *mrita* "mortal." The Greek word *ambrosia* is cognate and has the same meanings: *amrita* is the ambrosia of the gods, the drink that makes them live forever, and in a general sense it means sweet or nectarlike. So the

translation could also be "your words, which are like ambrosia."

22 The mind (*manas*) is here taken to be one of the senses or indriyas of perception; for example, it is really with the mind rather than with the eye that we see.

33 The Sanskrit alphabet, too, begins with the letter *a*; perhaps this is why Krishna declares that among letters he is *a,* the first. Another possible reason is that *a* is the most frequent sound in Sanskrit.

CHAPTER ELEVEN

14 Here Arjuna presses the palms of his hands together in the gesture called *anjali,* like one of the commonest Western gestures of prayer. This is the usual form of respectful greeting in India, as well as being used in worship and prayer.

15 Brahma, the Creator (not to be confused with Brahman, the attributeless Godhead, which is beyond the Trinity of creation, preservation, and destruction) sits within a lotus that grows from the navel of Lord Vishnu.

17 Here Arjuna sees not his friend Krishna, but the Lord incarnate in Krishna: Vishnu, armed with his traditional weapons, a club (or mace) and a discus. Not mentioned in this verse are the two benign symbols he carries in his other two hands, a conch and a lotus.

CHAPTER TWELVE

1 Arjuna is asking which path is superior, that of knowledge (jnana yoga) or love (bhakti yoga).

CHAPTER THIRTEEN

5 This is a list of all the twenty-four categories given

in Sankhya philosophy to describe phenomena in the field of prakriti.

CHAPTER FIFTEEN

1 The ashvattha is the sacred pipal tree, a kind of fig often grown in temple compounds in India. The idea of a "world tree" appears in many ancient cultures. Here the Gita uses the image of the tree as "upside down," drawing on the fact that the pipal sends out aerial roots, making "branches above and below." The image illustrates the phenomenal world, rooted in Brahman, complete unity, and branching out into the apparent diversity of life as it is ordinarily perceived.

13 *Rasatmaka soma* is here translated as "life-giving fluid," the nourishment of plants. In Hindu mythology it is the moon, sometimes called Soma, that nourishes plants, as the source of the life-giving nectar called Soma. In the Vedas, soma is an intoxicating, invigorating drink distilled from a plant grown high in the mountains and drunk by participants in a sacred ritual. Scholars have tried to discover what the soma plant might have been, but so far no conclusive identification has been made. Soma also appears as an important god in the Vedas.

CHAPTER SEVENTEEN

27–28 *Sat* means that which is real or true and that which is good; it derives from the Sanskrit verb *as,* to be, and is directly related to our English word *is.* It is noteworthy that this word *sat* links reality and goodness, reflecting the idea that good is eternal; it is merely covered from time to time by *asat,* evil, which is temporary and in that sense unreal. *Asat* is formed from *sat* by the addition of the prefix *a* "without," very much the way English forms words like *amoral.*

CHAPTER EIGHTEEN

1 *Sannyasa* and *tyaga* both mean renunciation, *sannyasa* from the root *as* "to cast aside" and *tyaga* from *tyaj* "to give up." The distinction between these two is clarified in the introduction to this chapter.

14 "The divine will" is a translation of *daivam,* which comes from the word *deva,* "god." *Daivam* is sometimes translated as "fate," but this is inappropriate in the Gita, which is not at all fatalistic. The Gita does, however, allow a place for God's will or Providence in the affairs of humankind—though of course the dominant force is usually karma, not daivam.

34 This verse uses the phrase *dharma-kama-artha,* "duty, pleasure, and wealth," traditionally considered the three goals of ordinary human life. The fourth and highest goal is *moksha,* salvation. The rajasic personality, as this verse points out, pursues the first three worldly goals; moksha is ignored.

41 The Vedas laid down the fourfold division of society into the classes of brahmin, kshatriya, vaishya, and shudra—roughly priests and intellectuals; warriors and rulers; businessmen, farmers, and craftsmen; and workers and servants.

66 *Dharma* is not used here in the usual sense of law or inner nature, but in a rarer meaning: a thing's attribute, condition, or conditioning. Usually *dharma* is used in this sense only in the plural, as here: thus dharma is divine law; dharmas are the innumerable beings, things, emotions and mental states that make up everyday existence as we experience it. Here, following the root meaning (*dhri,* to support or hold up), *sarva-dharman* is translated as "all your supports," in the sense of external props, con-

ditioned dependencies. Krishna means "cast off your dependency on everything external, Arjuna, and rely on the Self alone."

Glossary & Guide to Sanskrit Pronunciation

Consonants. Consonants are generally pronounced as in English, but there are some differences. Sanskrit has many so-called aspirated consonants, that is, consonants pronounced with a slight *h* sound. For example, the consonant *ph* is pronounced as English *p* followed by an *h* as in ha*ph*azard; *bh* is as in a*bh*or. The aspirated consonants are *kh, gh, ch, jh, th, dh, ph, bh.*

h	as in	*h*ome
g	" "	*g*old
j	" "	*J*une

The other consonants are approximately as in English.

Vowels. Every Sanskrit vowel has two forms, one short and one long. The long form is pronounced twice as long as the short. In the English transliteration the long vowels are marked with a bar (¯). The diphthongs—*e, ai, o, au*—are also pronounced twice as long as the short vowels. Thus, in the words *nīla* "blue" and *gopa* "cowherd," the first syllable is held twice as long as the second.

a	as in	*u*p		*ri*	as in	w*ri*tten
ā	" "	f*a*ther		*e*	" "	th*ey*
i	" "	g*i*ve		*ai*	" "	*ai*sle
ī	" "	s*ee*		*o*	" "	g*o*
u	" "	p*u*t		*au*	" "	c*ow*
ū	" "	r*u*le				

GLOSSARY

THE SPELLING OF SANSKRIT WORDS

To simplify the spelling of Sanskrit words we have used a minimum of diacritical marks, retaining only the long mark (¯) for the long vowels and omitting the other diacritics which are sometimes used in rendering Sanskrit words into English. Some subtleties of Sanskrit pronunciation, such as the difference between retroflex and dental consonants, are therefore lost. The gain in simplicity, however, seems to outweigh this loss.

Glossary

adharma "Not dharma." Injustice, evil, anything which goes against moral laws.

advaita Having no duality; the supreme Reality, which is the "One without a second." The word *advaita* is especially used in Vēdanta philosophy, which stresses the unity of the Self (Ātman) and Brahman.

ahamkāra [*aham* "I"; *kāra* "maker"] Self-will, separateness.

ahimsā [*a* "not"; *himsā* "violence"] Nonviolence, doing no injury, wishing no harm.

ākāsha Space, sky; the most subtle of the five elements.

akshara The eternal; the syllable *Om*.

Ananta The cosmic serpent on which Vishnu reclines in rest.

apara ["not transcendent"] Lower knowledge; intellectual knowledge.

Arjuna One of the five Pāndava brothers and an important figure in Indian epic and legend. He is Srī Krishna's beloved disciple and friend in the Bhagavad Gītā.

Aryaman "The noble one," a Vedic god revered as an ancestor of mankind.

asat [*a* "not"; *sat* "truth, goodness"] Untruth; anything unreal, untrue, or lacking in goodness.

ashvattha The pipal tree, a kind of fig; it is regarded as holy and often grows in temple compounds.

Ashvatthāma A great archer and warrior, who is Drŏna's son.

asura In Hindu myth, a demon; figuratively, a being
    with an evil nature.
Ātman "Self"; the innermost soul in every creature,
    which is divine.
avatāra [*ava* "down"; *tri* "to cross"] The descent of God
    to earth; the incarnation of Vishnu on earth; the
    birth of divine consciousness in the human heart.
avidyā [*a* "not"; *vidyā* "wisdom"] Ignorance, lack of
    wisdom, want of knowledge.
avyaya The eternal, the changeless.
Bhagavad Gītā [*Bhagavat* "lord"; *gītā* "song"] "The
    Song of the Lord," name of a Hindu scripture
    which contains the instructions of Srī Krishna.
bhakti Devotion, worship, love.
bhakti yoga The Way of Love.
Bhīshma A revered elder of the Kaurava dynasty who
    allows himself to be killed by Arjuna in the
    Mahābhārata battle.
Brahmā God as creator, one of the Hindu Trinity; the
    others are Vishnu, the Preserver, and Shiva, the
    Destroyer. *Brahmā,* a word with masculine gender,
    should not be confused with *Brahman,* which has
    neuter gender. (See entry below.)
brahmachārya "Conduct leading to God," self-control,
    purity.
Brahman The supreme reality underlying all life, the
    divine ground of existence, the impersonal God-
    head.
brahmanirvāna "Nirvana in Brahman," the final state of
    spiritual fulfillment: eternal union with Brahman,
    the ground of all being.
Brahmavidyā The science of knowing Brahman.
brahmin [Skt. *brāhmana*] Literally, a person who strives
    to know Brahman; in traditional Hindu society, a
    person of the priestly or learned class.
Bhrigu A sage famous in ancient legend.
Brihaspati The guru or priest of the gods.

Buddha [from *budh* "to wake up"] "The Awakened one," the title given to the sage Siddhārtha Gautama Shākyamuni after he obtained complete illumination. The Buddha lived and taught in North India during the sixth century B.C.

buddhi Understanding, intelligence; the faculty of discrimination; correct view, idea, purpose.

Chitraratha "Having a bright chariot," the name of the king of Gandharvas.

daivam Divine will; destiny.

deva A divine being, a god. The devas of Hindu mythology resemble the Olympians of the ancient Greeks—extraordinary, immortal, yet not unlike mortal men and women in their behavior. The feminine is *devī*, "goddess."

dharma Law, duty; the universal law which holds all life together in unity.

Dhritarāshtra The king of the Kurus. He has been blind since birth and has therefore never been enthroned as the rightful king, but he serves as de facto ruler. The entire Bhagavad Gītā is a narration told by Sanjaya to the blind king, whose sons are the Kauravas.

Draupadī The royal princess who became the wife of each of the five Pāndava brothers.

Drona A learned brahmin who became a warrior, and eventually general of the Kaurava army. The preceptor of the royal princes, he taught the heroes of the *Mahābhārata* the skills of war.

duhkha Pain, suffering, sorrow.

Duryodhana The oldest son of Dhritarāshtra and the chief enemy of the Pāndavas and Srī Krishna.

dvandva In Sanskrit grammar, a kind of compound word that combines two or more words as a pair or group.

Gandharva Heavenly musicians who are demigods, rather touchy and proud, handsome and amorous.

Gāndīva The name of Arjuna's bow, which was a gift
    from the god of fire.

Ganges [Skt. *gangā*] A major river of northern India,
    looked upon as a sacred symbol.

Garuda The great eagle that is Vishnu's vehicle.

gāyatrī A kind of meter used in the Vedic hymns; a
    prayer to the sun composed in this meter.

Gītā "The Song," a shorter title for the Bhagavad Gītā.

guna Quality; specifically, the three qualities which
    make up the phenomenal world: *sattva,* law, har-
    mony, purity, goodness; *rajas,* energy, passion; and
    tamas, inertia, ignorance. The corresponding adjec-
    tives are *sattvic, rajasic,* and *tamasic.*

guru A spiritual teacher.

Hastināpura "City of the elephants," an important city
    in ancient India, located about sixty miles northeast
    of the modern Delhi. It was the capital of the Pān-
    davas and their line.

Hari Name of Vishnu or Krishna.

Himālaya [*hima* "snow"; *alaya* "abode"] The great
    mountain range which stretches across the northern
    border of India, important in mythology as the
    home of Shiva and other gods.

Ikshvāku The son of Manu, and founder of the great
    Solar Dynasty of kings.

Indra The god of storms and battle. In the Veda, Indra is
    the chief of the gods (devas) and an important deity;
    later his role is greatly diminished.

Īshvara The Lord; God.

Janaka A king of ancient times who was both an effec-
    tive ruler and a holy sage.

Janārdana "He who stirs up the people," name of Krishna.

jīva Living being; the living soul; the finite, individual
    soul that is identified with separate existence, as
    opposed to Ātman, the eternal Self.

jnāna [from *jnā* "to know"] Wisdom; higher know-
    ledge.

jnāna yoga The Way of Wisdom.

kālpa A period in cosmic time equaling one Day of Brahmā or 1,000 "great yugas"—a total of 4,320 million years. See also *yuga*.

kāma Selfish desire, greed; sexual desire, sometimes personified as Kāmadeva.

Kāmadhuk "The cow of wishes," who in legend fulfills all desires.

Kapila Name of a sage, first teacher of the Sānkhya philosophy.

karma [from *kri* "to do"] Action; former actions which will lead to certain results in a cause-and-effect relationship.

karma yoga The Way of Action; the path of selfless service.

Karna A brave warrior who plays an important role in the larger epic, but is only mentioned in passing in the Gītā.

Kauravas "The sons of Kuru," Duryodhana and his brothers, who are the enemies of the Pāndava brothers.

Kripa A revered teacher of the royal family who also serves as a warrior.

Krishna ['black'; or from *krish* 'to draw, to attract to oneself'] "The Dark One" or "He who draws us to Himself," name of an incarnation of Vishnu. Vishnu, the cosmic force of goodness, comes to earth as Krishna to re-establish dharma, or law. Krishna is the friend and advisor of the Pāndava brothers, especially Arjuna, to whom he reveals the teachings of the Bhagavad Gītā. He is the inner Lord, who personifies spiritual love and lives in the hearts of all beings.

kshatriya A warrior or prince; a member of the ruling class of traditional Hindu society.

kshetra A field; a place; a sacred place or temple.

Kubera God of wealth.

kundalinī "The serpent power," spiritual or evolutionary energy. In yoga literature, kundalinī is
  described as a force coiled at the base of the spine.
  Kundalinī may be aroused through meditation and
  the practice of yoga; then it rises up through the
  subtle body, awakening the higher centers of consciousness.

Kurukshetra "The field of the Kurus," where the
  Mahābhārata battle takes place. It is north of the
  modern city of Delhi.

līlā Game; the divine play of the Lord disguising himself as the many beings of this world.

Mādhava Another name for Krishna, "the descendant
  of Madhu."

Madhusūdana "Slayer of Madhu," a name for Krishna,
  who killed the demon Madhu.

Mahābhārata Name of the great Indian epic composed
  some 2,500 years ago, traditionally attributed to the
  sage Vyāsa. It relates the conflict between the de-
  scendants of Pāndu (the forces of light) and those of
  Dhritarāshtra (the forces of darkness).

manas The mind; specifically, the faculty which registers and stores sensory impressions.

mantram [or *mantra*] A Holy Name or phrase; a spiritual
  formula.

Manu The father of the human race, the Hindu equivalent of Adam or the first man.

Mārgashīrsha The lunar month that falls in November–
  December.

Marīchi A Vedic demigod. The name means "particle
  of light."

Māyā Illusion; appearance, as contrasted with Reality;
  the creative power of God.

Meru A mythical mountain said to stand at the center of
  the world or cosmos. The gods dwell on Meru in
  beautiful cities, amidst flowering gardens.

Mīrā A woman saint of medieval India remembered for her songs to her beloved Krishna.

moksha Liberation, salvation, illumination.

Nakula One of the junior Pāndava brothers.

Nārada The divine musician and sage who is a devotee of Srī Krishna.

Nirvāna [*nir* "out"; *vāna* "to blow"] Complete extinction of self-will and separateness; realization of the unity of all life. (See also Notes, p.216.)

nirvikalpa samādhi A state of spiritual awareness in which there is no perception of duality, of inside or outside, of subject and object; merger in the impersonal Godhead.

Om [or *Aum*] The cosmic sound, heard in deep meditation; the Holy Word, taught in the Upanishads, which signifies Brahman, the divine ground of existence.

Pāndavas "The sons of Pāndu," a collective name for Arjuna and his four brothers, Yudhishthira, Bhīma, Nakula, and Sahadeva. The Pāndavas are in conflict with the Kauravas; both claim the ancient throne of Hastināpura. The Gītā is placed on the eve of the battle that will decide this conflict. The Pāndavas are looked upon as the forces for good and the Kauravas as wicked usurpers, greedy for wealth and power.

Pārtha "Son of Prithā," a name for Arjuna–or for his brothers Bhīma and Yudhishthira.

Patanjali The author of the *Yoga Sūtras,* a classic description of the way to Self-realization through meditation. Patanjali lived around the second century B.C., and his method is sometimes referred to as *rāja yoga.*

Pāvaka "The purifier," a name for the god of fire.

Prahlāda A demon prince who was greatly devoted to Vishnu.

Prajāpati "lord of offspring," the creator of all beings. Indian myth encompasses many creation stories, and sometimes one great Father, or Prajāpati, is mentioned; sometimes there are seven or more fathers or sages who created all living creatures.

prajñā [from *jñā* "to know"] A transcendental mode of knowing developed in deep meditation.

prakriti The basic energy from which the mental and physical worlds take shape; nature.

prāna Breath; vital force.

Prithā Arjuna's mother (also called Kuntī). Arjuna is called Pārtha, "son of Prithā."

Purusha ["person"] The soul; the spiritual core of every person. In the Gītā, the terms *Ātman* and *Purusha* are virtually interchangeable.

Purushottama "Highest Person," Supreme Being, God.

rāja yoga "The Royal Path"; the path of meditation taught especially by Patanjali in the *Yoga Sūtras*.

rajas See under *guna*.

Rāma "Prince of Joy," name of the son of Dasharatha, who was king of Ayodhyā. Rāma was the famous prince who killed the evil demon Ravana to reclaim his wife Sītā. He is regarded as an incarnation of Vishnu.

Rig Veda The oldest of the four Vedas, which are the most ancient and sacred of the Hindu scriptures.

Rudras A group of gods associated with storm and destruction. Sometimes the Rudras are mentioned as a group; at other times they are thought of as a single god, Rudra. In later Hinduism, Shiva is called Rudra.

sādhana A body of disciplines or way of life which leads to the supreme goal of Self-realization.

sādhu A holy man, sage.

Sahadeva One of the junior Pāndava brothers.

Sāma Veda The Veda of songs and chants. One of the four Vedas.

234

samādhi Mystical union with God; a state of intense concentration in which consciousness is completely unified.

samsāra The world of flux; the round of birth, decay, death and rebirth.

Sanjaya The sage who divinely perceives the narrative of the Gītā and reports it to the blind king Dhrita-rāshtra.

Sānkhya One of the six branches of traditional Hindu philosophy. Sānkhya seeks to liberate the individual *Purusha* (spirit) from *prakriti* (mind and matter) through the knowledge of the ultimate separation of these two realities.

sannyāsa Renunciation.

sat [from *as* "to be"] The Real; truth; goodness.

sattva See under *guna*.

satya Truth, truthful; good, the Good.

savikalpa samādhi [*sa-vikalpa* "having distinctions" or "admitting separateness"] Samādhi in which some duality of subject and object remains, the devotee being absorbed in his meditation without becoming completely identified with the object of contemplation; union with the personal God.

Shakti Power; God's feminine aspect; the Divine Mother.

shama Peace; the peace of deep meditation.

Shankara "Giver of peace," a name of Shiva.

Shiva The third Person of the Hindu Trinity, the other two being Brahmā, the Creator, and Vishnu, the preserver. Shiva destroys, but he also conquers death.

shraddhā Faith.

shūdra The fourth Hindu caste; a worker or servant.

Skanda A god of war, the son of Shiva; general of the divine forces when they go into battle against the demons.

soma A drink used in Vedic ritual; the drink of the gods.

Srī [pronounced *shrī*] A title of respect originally
    meaning "lord" or "holy."
svadharma The duty appropriate to a particular person,
    one's own individual dharma.
tamas See under *guna*.
tapas Austerity, control of the senses; the spiritual
    power acquired through self-control.
tyāga Renunciation.
Upanishads Ancient mystical documents found at the
    end of each of the four vedas.
Ushanas A sage and poet who appears in the Vedas.
varna Caste or class; specifically, one of the four general
    classes of traditional Hindu society.
Varuna God of waters and the ocean; in the Veda, the
    moral overseer of the world.
Vāsuki The king of the serpents, he lives in the under-
    world and balances the earth on his serpent hood.
Veda [from *vid* "to know"] "Knowledge"; the name of
    the most ancient Sanskrit scriptures, considered to
    be a direct revelation from God to the mystics of the
    past.
vidyā Knowledge, wisdom; a science or branch of
    study.
vijnāna Knowledge, judgment, understanding.
Vishnu Second in the Hindu Trinity; the Preserver who
    incarnates himself in age after age for the establish-
    ment of dharma and for the welfare of all creatures.
Vivasvat The sun god, the father of Manu, the ancestor
    of mankind.
Vrishni Name of an important clan of ancient north
    India. According to legend the Vrishnis all perished
    at the end of Krishna's life when their city, Dvāraka,
    sank in the sea.
Vyāsa The sage revered as the author of the Mahābhār-
    ata and the Gītā. He was the father of both Dhrita-
    rāshtra and Pāndu, and he gave Sanjaya the power

of mystic vision so that he could behold the dialogue between Srī Krishna and Arjuna.

yajna Offering, sacrifice, worship.

Yajur One of the four Vedas.

yoga [from *yuj* "to unite"] Union with God, realization of the unity of all life; a path or discipline which leads to such a state of total integration or unity. Yoga is also the name of one of the six branches of Hindu philosophy, and as such is paired with Sānkhya.

yogī A person who practices spiritual disciplines.

Yudhishthira Arjuna's elder brother, who is famous for his adherence to dharma at all times.

yuga An age or eon. In Hindu cosmology there are four yugas, representing a steady deterioration in the state of the world from age to age. The names of the yugas are taken from a game of dice. Krita yuga is the age of perfection, followed by tretā yuga. The incarnation of Srī Krishna is said to mark the end of the third yuga, dvāpara. We are living in the fourth and final yuga, kali, in which the creation reaches its lowest point. The world goes through 1,000 such yuga-cycles during one kalpa or Day of Brahma.

Index

239

END

Library of Congress Cataloging in Publication Data

Bhagavadgītā.   English.
    The Bhagavad Gita.

    I.   Easwaran, Eknath.   II.   Title.
BL1138.6.B4513   1985   294.5'924   85–10637
ISBN 0–915132–36–2
ISBN 0–915132–35–4 (pbk.)